JAMESTOWN  EDUCATION

MW01124216

The Real Deal
Danger Zone

Henry Billings
Melissa Billings

 Glencoe

New York, New York   Columbus, Ohio   Chicago, Illinois   Peoria, Illinois   Woodland Hills, California

Reviewers

Kati Pearson
Reading Specialist/Literacy Coach
Carver Middle School
4500 West Columbia Street
Orlando, FL 32811

Suzanne Zweig
Reading Specialist
Sullivan High School
6631 North Bosworth Avenue
Chicago, IL 60626

Beth Dalton
Reading Consultant
Los Angeles County Office of
Education
9300 Imperial Avenue
Downey, CA 90240

Carolyn S. Reid
Reading Specialist
Alief Hastings High School
12301 High Star
Houston, TX 77072

Glencoe

The *McGraw-Hill* Companies

ISBN: 0-07-861695-6

Send all queries to:
Glencoe/McGraw-Hill
8787 Orion Place
Columbus, OH 43240-4027

1 2 3 4 5 6 7 8 9   024   09 08 07 06 05 04

Contents

Unit Three

To the Student

Some people face danger in their work—treating victims of a deadly virus, rescuing trapped climbers from the peaks of mountains, or fishing in the rough waters of the Bering Sea. Others choose dangerous hobbies—skeleton racing, free diving, adventure racing, or BASE jumping. There are 13 true stories in this book. In them you will meet people who enter the danger zone in a variety of ways.

As you do the lessons in this book, you will improve your reading skills. This will help you increase your reading comprehension. You also will improve your thinking skills. The lessons include types of questions often found on state and national tests. Working with these questions will help you prepare for tests you may have to take in the future.

How to Use This Book

About the Book. *Danger Zone* has three units. Each one has four lessons. Each lesson starts with a true story. The stories are about people who show courage in the face of danger. Each story is followed by a group of seven exercises. They test comprehension and thinking skills. They will help you understand and think about what you read. At the end of the lesson, you can give your personal response. You can also rate how well you understood what you read.

The Sample Lesson. The first lesson in the book is a sample. It explains how to complete the questions. It also shows how to score your answers. The correct answers are printed in lighter type. In some cases, the reasons an answer is correct are given. Studying these reasons will help you learn how to think through the questions. You might have questions about how to do the exercises or score them. If so, you should ask those questions now, before you start Unit One.

Working Through Each Lesson. Start each lesson by looking at the photo. Next read the caption. Before you read the story, guess what you think it will be about. Then read the story.

After you finish the story, do the exercises. Study the directions for each exercise. They will tell you how to mark your answers. Do all seven exercises. Then check your work. Your teacher will give you an answer key to do this. Follow the directions after each exercise to find your score. At the end of the lesson, add up your total score. Record that score on the graph on page 115.

At the end of each unit, you will complete a Compare and Contrast Chart. The chart will help you see what some of the stories in that unit have in common. It will also help you explore your own ideas about the events in the stories.

Sample Lesson

The Running of the Bulls

Al Chesson had been lucky. Eleven times he "ran with the bulls." Eleven times he did it safely. But on July 8, 2003, his luck ran out. A bull caught the 57-year-old man and pierced him with its horn three times.

2 Chesson didn't get paid to put his life in danger. No one made him do it. He did it because he loved it. To him, it was fun. He said running with the bulls was as exciting as being in a battle.

3 Chesson is not alone. Every year hundreds of people run with the bulls. They want to test their luck. They want to see how brave they are. They know they might get hurt or they might even die. Since 1924 the bulls have killed more than a dozen people. But this doesn't stop others from running.

4 The running of the bulls takes place in Pamplona, Spain. Each July, people flock to this small town. They come for the Fiesta de San Fermin. The holiday lasts eight days. It includes many bullfights. Bullfighting is an old custom in Spain. Special bulls are raised there for this purpose. The bulls weigh as much as 1,300 pounds.

Runners try to dodge the racing bulls during the first bull run of the annual festival in Pamplona, Spain.

And these bulls are tough. They have been known to attack anything that moves.

5 The bulls in Pamplona are kept in a corral. This is an area surrounded by high fences. The corral is 900 yards from the bullring where the bullfight takes place. For each day's fights, six bulls are needed. So six of them are let out of the corral every day. They charge through the streets and into the ring. This is called the "running of the bulls."

6 People who want to test their courage run ahead of the animals. Others watch from buildings. Still others watch from behind wooden walls that are put up just for this event. The runners are easy to spot. They wear white pants and T-shirts. They also wear red strips of cloth around their necks and around their waists. Most of the runners are male.

7 There are rules for running with the bulls. Runners can't carry anything that would hurt the bulls. They can't jump out of hiding places. They can't grab the bulls. They also can't block a bull in any way. The only things the runners can carry are rolled-up newspapers. The very bravest wave them to catch a bull's eye. It is exciting for them to know they have a bull's attention.

8 A rocket goes off to signal the start of the running. Then a wild dash through the streets begins. The bulls run faster than people. So runners have to jump out of

the way as the bulls pass them. The worst thing a runner can do is trip and fall. That is what happened to Matthew Tassio. In 1995 he was running ahead of the bulls. Then he fell. Before Tassio stood up, a bull got him. One of its horns caught him in the stomach. Within minutes, Tassio died.

9   No one knows for sure what angry bulls will do. When they get confused, they take their fear out on anyone around them. That is why six or seven oxen are sent through the streets with the bulls. The oxen are gentle farm animals. They keep the bulls running in the right direction. But some bulls still get confused. The most dangerous bull is one who gets turned around.

10   Anton Rose saw a bull get turned around in 2003. He and some friends were running with the bulls. They reached a place called "death corner." This is a sharp turn where bulls often slip and fall. When the bulls get up, they may go the wrong way. When one bull got to its feet, it came right at Rose.

11   "The bull turned around and looked at me," said Rose. "I thought I was done for. We all did." Luckily, Rose reached safety. So did his friends. They scrambled over a wooden wall and away from the angry bull.

12   Al Chesson's story had a different ending. He had almost reached the bullring when a bull spun around and came at him.

13   "He took one look and came right at me," said Chesson.

14   It all happened very fast. Chesson didn't even have time to be afraid. He fell to the ground. He hoped the bull would move on and charge someone else. But it stayed with him. The animal hit Chesson three times in the leg and lower body. Then it flung him into the air. The bull was like a giant tossing coins. "He kept lifting me . . . with his horns," Chesson said. "You really don't have much control once he gets you."

15   That was Al Chesson's last running of the bulls. He said he would return to Spain. He loves the country. And he loves the people. But never again will he put himself in the path of an angry Pamplona bull. ✖

A. Finding the Main Idea

One statement below tells the main idea of the article. One statement is too general, or too broad. The other statement explains only part of the article; it is too narrow. Label the statements using the following key:

M—Main Idea   **B—Too Broad**   **N—Too Narrow**

B   1. People sometimes put themselves in danger just for the fun of it. [This statement is true, but it is *too broad.* It does not tell which danger these people are putting themselves into.]

N   2. Al Chesson could have died when a bull caught up to him. The bull hurt him badly and tossed him in the air. [This statement is true, but it is *too narrow.* It gives only a few facts from the article.]

M   3. Every year hundreds of people test their courage in a special event in Spain. They run ahead of bulls on their way to the bullring. [This statement is the *main idea.* It tells you that the article is about the people who run with the bulls in Spain. It also tells where the bulls are running.]

Score 4 points for each correct answer.

_____ **Total Score:** Finding the Main Idea

B. Recalling Facts

How well do you remember the facts in the article? Put an X in the box next to the answer that correctly completes each statement.

1. The Fiesta de San Fermin takes place in
   - ☐ a. January.
   - ☒ b. July.
   - ☐ c. October.

2. The corral where the bulls are kept before the bullfight is
   - ☒ a. 900 yards from the bullring.
   - ☐ b. 100 yards from the bullring.
   - ☐ c. two miles from the bullring.

3. The oxen run with the bulls to
   - ☐ a. make the bulls angry.
   - ☐ b. make the run more exciting.
   - ☒ c. keep the bulls running the right way.

4. Runners wear
   - ☐ a. yellow pants, red T-shirts, and white strips of cloth.
   - ☐ b. red pants and T-shirts and white strips of cloth.
   - ☒ c. white pants and T-shirts and red strips of cloth.

Score 4 points for each correct answer.

_____ **Total Score:** Recalling Facts

C. Making Inferences

When you draw a conclusion that is not directly stated in the text, you are making an inference. Put an X in the box next to the statement that is a correct inference.

1.

☒ a. People in Pamplona spend time getting ready for the running of the bulls every year.

☐ b. No one outside Pamplona ever heard of the custom of the running of the bulls.

☐ c. The running of the bulls is more dangerous for the bulls than it is for the runners.

2.

☐ a. If people knew that others had died running with the bulls, no one would do it.

☒ b. You have to be a good, fast runner to run with the bulls safely.

☐ c. Only people who live in Spain are allowed to run with the bulls.

Score 4 points for each correct answer.

_____ **Total Score:** Making Inferences

D. Using Words

Put an X in the box next to the definition below that is closest in meaning to the underlined word.

1. The clerk <u>pierced</u> her ears so she could put rings through them.

☒ a. put a hole in
☐ b. covered with a hat
☐ c. colored

2. People <u>flock</u> to the ball park to see games they think their team might win.

☐ a. stay away
☒ b. come together
☐ c. pretend not to see

3. We like marching in parades. It is our <u>custom</u> to have a parade on this day every year.

☒ a. something people have done for years
☐ b. something to be afraid of
☐ c. something no one thought would happen

4. Happy fans sometimes knock down people and things when they <u>charge</u> onto a field.

☐ a. wander slowly
☐ b. walk as if in a dream
☒ c. rush with force

5. The children <u>scrambled</u> up the hill on their hands and knees until they reached the top.

- ☐ a. ran quickly
- ☒ b. climbed or crawled
- ☐ c. held tight

6. Everyone stood back when Dad <u>flung</u> a heavy log onto the fire.

- ☐ a. picked up
- ☐ b. sawed in two
- ☒ c. threw hard

Score 4 points for each correct answer.

_____ **Total Score:** Using Words

E. Author's Approach

Put an X in the box next to the correct answer.

1. The author uses the first sentence of the article to

- ☒ a. make readers wonder what made Al Chesson lucky.
- ☐ b. describe how Al Chesson looked and sounded.
- ☐ c. compare Al Chesson and Matthew Tassio.

2. What is the author's purpose in writing this article?

- ☐ a. to get the reader to run with the bulls in Pamplona
- ☐ b. to describe the sport of bullfighting in Spain
- ☒ c. to tell what happens at the running of the bulls

3. From the statements below, choose the one that you believe the author would agree with.

- ☐ a. Everyone should go to Spain to run with the bulls every year.
- ☐ b. People who run with the bulls are being cruel to the bulls.
- ☒ c. Running with the bulls is a dangerous thing to do.

Score 4 points for each correct answer.

_____ **Total Score:** Author's Approach

F. Summarizing and Paraphrasing

Put an X in the box next to the correct answer.

1. Which summary says all the important things about the article?

☐ a. Runners in Pamplona, Spain, often fall down. The bulls can catch up to the runners and hurt them. [This summary leaves out most important details.]

☐ b. People come to Pamplona, Spain, every July. They have fun at the the Fiesta de San Fermin. [This summary presents some important details from the article but misses too many others.]

☒ c. The running of the bulls takes place every July in Pamplona, Spain. Brave people can get hurt or killed when they run ahead of bulls to the bullring. [This summary says all the most important things.]

2. Which sentence means the same thing as the following sentence? "The very bravest wave them [rolled-up newspapers] to catch a bull's eye."

☐ a. The bravest runners put bulls' eyes in newspapers.

☒ b. The bravest runners wave rolled-up newspapers to make a bull look at them. ["To make a bull look at them" means the same thing as "to catch a bull's eye."]

☐ c. Some brave runners wave newspapers at each other.

Score 4 points for each correct answer.

_____ **Total Score:** Summarizing and Paraphrasing

G. Critical Thinking

Put an X in the box next to the correct answer.

1. Choose the statement below that states a fact.

☐ a. Running with the bulls is a silly way to have fun.

☐ b. People should stop fighting bulls because it is cruel.

☒ c. Matthew Tassio tripped and fell in front of a bull in 1995.

2. From information in the article, you can predict that

☒ a. people in Pamplona will keep having the running of the bulls as long as they can.

☐ b. if anyone else gets hurt, the running of the bulls will not be held anymore.

☐ c. people will get tired of the running of the bulls very soon.

3. Al Chesson and Matthew Tassio are different because

☐ a. only Chesson was hurt by a bull.

☐ b. only Tassio fell before the bull caught up to him.

☒ c. only Tassio was killed by a bull.

4. Which paragraphs provide information that supports your answer to question 3?

☐ a. paragraphs 9, 10, and 11

☒ b. paragraphs 8, 14, and 15

☐ c. paragraphs 1, 2, and 3

5. How is running with the bulls an example of going into the danger zone?

☐ a. Hundreds of runners take part in the event every year.

☐ b. Runners wear clothes that set them apart from the rest of the crowd.

☒ c. Runners can get hurt or even killed.

Score 4 points for each correct answer.

_____ **Total Score:** Critical Thinking

Enter your score for each activity. Add the scores together. Record your total score on the graph on page 115.

_____ Finding the Main Idea

_____ Recalling Facts

_____ Making Inferences

_____ Using Words

_____ Author's Approach

_____ Summarizing and Paraphrasing

_____ Critical Thinking

_____ **Total Score**

Personal Response

If you could ask the author of the article one question, what would it be? [Do you want to know how the author learned so much about the topic? Do you want to know any details that the author did not talk about? Write one question on the lines.]

_____

_____

Self-Assessment

A word or phrase in the article that I do not understand is

_____

[Look over the article. Find a word or a group of words that gave you trouble. Write it on the line.]

Self-Assessment

You can take charge of your own progress. Here are some features to help you focus on your progress in learning reading and thinking skills.

Personal Response and Self-Assessment. These questions help you connect the stories to your life. They help you think about your understanding of what you have read.

Comprehension and Critical Thinking Progress Graph. A graph at the end of the book helps you to keep track of your progress. Check the graph often with your teacher. Together, decide whether you need more work on some skills. What types of skills cause you trouble? Talk with your teacher about ways to work on these.

A sample Progress Graph is shown on the right. The first three lessons have been filled in to show you how to use the graph.

Comprehension and Critical Thinking Progress Graph

Directions: Write your score for each lesson in the box under the number of the lesson. Then put a small X on the line directly above the number of the lesson and across from the score you earned. Chart your progress by drawing a line to connect the Xs.

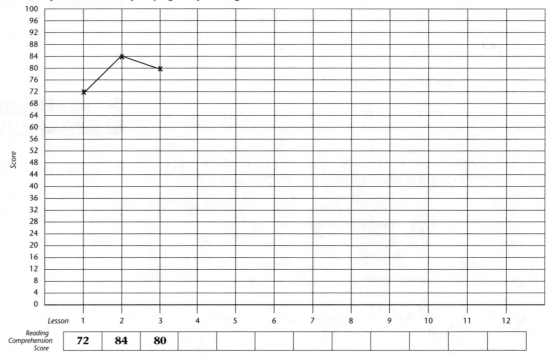

Lesson	1	2	3	4	5	6	7	8	9	10	11	12
Reading Comprehension Score	72	84	80									

UNIT ONE

Flight to Freedom

Alina Fernandez hated living in Cuba. Life was hard there. Food was scarce. So was medicine. Most people had no cars. Fernandez had a car, but she could not get much gas for it. Even books were hard to get in this poor country.

2   Fernandez dreamed of leaving Cuba. In 1986 she tried to go to Mexico. But the Cuban government would not let her. Five years later, she tried to go to Spain. Again, government workers said no. "You're not going anywhere," they told her. "You're going to die right here with the rest of us."

3   Fernandez believed them. She did not think she would ever get out of Cuba. After all, her father was Fidel Castro. He was the leader of the country. He would never let Fernandez leave. It would make him look bad if his own child left Cuba behind.

4   So for many years, Fernandez stayed where she was. She worked at odd jobs. She took care of her daughter, Alina Maria. But she was not free. And she had no hope.

After escaping to the United States, Alina Fernandez, the daughter of Fidel Castro, appears at a news conference with her daughter, Alina Maria.

"Things were getting worse in Cuba every day," she said. "I imagined the future and it was empty. So was I."

5   By 1993 she could not take it anymore. She felt as if she had no purpose in life. And she feared that 16-year-old Alina Maria would soon feel the same way. "I was like a vegetable, and she was beginning to be one too," said Fernandez. "We had to get out."

6   Fernandez decided to sneak out of Cuba. It would be dangerous. If she were caught, she could be sent to jail. She might be beaten. She might be treated badly—or worse. But Fernandez was willing to take that chance. She was willing to do almost anything to get away.

7   There was just one thing she would not do. She would not put her daughter in danger. Fernandez longed to take Alina Maria out of Cuba. But if the girl came with her, they would both be breaking the law. If they were caught, Alina Maria might be severely punished. Fernandez would not let that happen. So she chose to sneak out alone. If she made it, she would try to get Alina Maria out legally.

8   Fernandez talked to a friend from Spain. The friend sent her a fake passport. A passport is a government paper. It allows a person to travel to other countries. The friend's passport showed a photograph of a Spanish woman. She was much larger than Fernandez. Her hair was much longer too. Fernandez wanted to pretend to

be that woman and use the passport. So she found a wig to wear. She also began to eat extra food to gain weight. She did everything she could to look more like the picture on the passport.

9   For two months, Fernandez built up her weight. She also built up her strength. She worked out in secret. She did sit-ups and push-ups. She ran in place. She knew she would need a strong mind and a strong body to carry out her daring plan.

10   At first, Fernandez did not want her daughter to know her plan. But as the time to leave drew near, she told Alina Maria the truth. "She was brave and kept the secret," Fernandez said. In fact, Alina Maria liked the plan. She wanted her mother to go. It gave her hope that someday she might get out too.

11   On December 19, 1993, Fernandez made her move. She put on the wig. She put on a tan coat. She also put on heavy makeup. The woman in the picture had big lips. "I made my mouth big with lots of lipstick," Fernandez said. Then she packed a small travel bag. It held things that a Spanish tourist might carry. This meant a bathing suit and a few other clothes. Fernandez could not take more. Taking too many clothes would look suspicious. She could not take anything that would reveal who she really was. She could not take even a picture of Alina Maria.

12   Saying goodbye to her daughter was not easy. Fernandez gave Alina Maria a hug.

13   "I love you," she said.

14   "I love you more," the girl replied.

15   At the airport, Fernandez tried to fit in with the tourists. She walked past the guards. Then she went to the gate. No one stopped her. Holding her breath, she boarded a plane bound for Spain. Eight and a half hours later, she landed in Spain. She had done it! She had escaped from Cuba. She asked the U. S. government to let her move to the United States. The U. S. government agreed. And so on December 21, she flew to Florida.

16   Word of Fernandez's escape spread quickly. Everyone thought Fidel Castro should let Alina Maria out too. He felt more and more pressed. After a few days, he gave in. On New Year's Eve, Alina Maria boarded a plane in Cuba. She flew to Florida, where she stepped into her mother's arms. At last, Fernandez and her daughter were out of the danger zone.

A. Finding the Main Idea

One statement below tells the main idea of the article. One statement is too general, or too broad. The other statement explains only part of the article; it is too narrow. Label the statements using the following key:

M—Main Idea   B—Too Broad   N—Too Narrow

_____ 1. Being the daughter of a famous man or woman sometimes can be fun. But if you ask Alina Fernandez, she would say that being a famous man's daughter is hard.

_____ 2. Fidel Castro's daughter, Alina Fernandez, used a fake passport to escape from Cuba. When Fernandez got to the United States, Castro allowed her daughter to join her.

_____ 3. Alina Fernandez put on heavy makeup before she boarded a plane to Spain. She wanted her lips to look bigger, so she put on plenty of lipstick.

Score 4 points for each correct answer.

_____ **Total Score:** Finding the Main Idea

B. Recalling Facts

How well do you remember the facts in the article? Put an X in the box next to the answer that correctly completes each statement.

1. Before 1993 Alina Fernandez had tried to run away to

☐ a. the United States and France.
☐ b. Mexico and Spain.
☐ c. England and Brazil.

2. Fernandez left her daughter behind when she left Cuba because

☐ a. her daughter loved Cuba too much to leave.
☐ b. her daughter was too busy to leave Cuba.
☐ c. she didn't want to put her daughter in danger.

3. To get ready to escape from Cuba, Fernandez

☐ a. gained weight and worked out.
☐ b. lost weight and shopped for new clothes.
☐ c. colored her hair black and learned to swim.

4. To get out of Cuba, Fernandez pretended to be

☐ a. a reporter from the United States.
☐ b. the daughter of Fidel Castro.
☐ c. a tourist from Spain.

Score 4 points for each correct answer.

_____ **Total Score:** Recalling Facts

C. Making Inferences

When you draw a conclusion that is not directly stated in the text, you are making an inference. Put an X in the box next to the statement that is a correct inference.

1.

☐ a. Fidel Castro and Alina Fernandez were very close. They let each other know everything they were thinking.

☐ b. Alina Fernandez loved her daughter more than words could say.

☐ c. Probably Alina Fernandez was the only Cuban who wanted to escape from Cuba.

2.

☐ a. Alina Fernandez was willing to work hard to get what she wanted.

☐ b. Alina Fernandez would never think of breaking any law.

☐ c. In 1993 tourists from Spain were not allowed to visit Cuba.

Score 4 points for each correct answer.

_____ **Total Score:** Making Inferences

D. Using Words

Put an X in the box next to the definition below that is closest in meaning to the underlined word.

1. During the war, gas was <u>scarce</u>, so people didn't drive their cars much.

☐ a. less costly than usual
☐ b. more than needed
☐ c. not enough to fill needs

2. Anyone who breaks the rules will be <u>severely</u> punished.

☐ a. in a way that causes pain
☐ b. in a happy way
☐ c. in a gentle, kind way

3. You cannot drive <u>legally</u> until you pass a driving test.

☐ a. in a way that goes against the law
☐ b. in a way allowed by the law
☐ c. in a way that leads to accidents

4. The <u>tourist</u> learned a few words of the language of each country she visited.

☐ a. a person who travels for fun
☐ b. a person who always stays at home
☐ c. a person who is kept in jail

5. The robber walked away slowly from the bank so police wouldn't think he looked <u>suspicious</u>.

  ☐ a. like a person who has done wrong

  ☐ b. like a person who has won a prize

  ☐ c. like a person who makes a lot of money

6. If you want to learn this trick, I will now <u>reveal</u> exactly how it is done.

  ☐ a. make a guess

  ☐ b. think deeply

  ☐ c. make known

Score 4 points for each correct answer.

_____ **Total Score:** Using Words

E. | Author's Approach

Put an X in the box next to the correct answer.

1. The main purpose of the first paragraph is to

  ☐ a. tell readers that Alina Fernandez was the daughter of the Cuban leader.

  ☐ b. tell how much gas Cubans could buy every week.

  ☐ c. explain why Alina Fernandez hated living in Cuba.

2. The author probably wrote this article in order to

  ☐ a. get airports to check passports more carefully.

  ☐ b. tell an exciting story.

  ☐ c. describe life in Spain.

3. The author tells this story mainly by

  ☐ a. telling what happened in time order.

  ☐ b. explaining different ideas.

  ☐ c. imagining what could have happened.

Score 4 points for each correct answer.

_____ **Total Score:** Author's Approach

F. Summarizing and Paraphrasing

Put an X in the box next to the correct answer.

1. Which summary says all the important things about the article?

☐ a. Alina Fernandez had been trying to escape from Cuba for years. Finally, in 1993 she used a fake passport and flew to Spain. Fidel Castro, her father and the leader of Cuba, let her daughter join her in the United States.

☐ b. Alina Fernandez flew to Spain in 1993. Then she went to the United States. A few days later, her daughter, Alina Maria, joined her in the United States.

☐ c. Alina Fernandez had a friend in Spain. That friend sent Fernandez a fake passport. Fernandez pretended to be the large woman with long hair pictured on the passport. Then she flew to Spain.

2. Which sentence means the same thing as the following sentence? "Holding her breath, she boarded a plane bound for Spain."

☐ a. She felt sick as she got onto the plane bound for Spain.

☐ b. She did not like the smell of the plane going to Spain, but she got on board anyway.

☐ c. She was nervous when she got on the plane going to Spain.

Score 4 points for each correct answer.

_____ **Total Score:** Summarizing and Paraphrasing

G. Critical Thinking

Put an X in the box next to the correct answer.

1. Choose the statement below that states a fact.

☐ a. No one should ever break any law, no matter how unfair the law is.

☐ b. Fernandez's flight to Spain took about eight and one-half hours.

☐ c. Castro did the right thing when he let Alina Maria join her mother in the United States.

2. Fernandez and the woman pictured on the passport were different because

☐ a. Fernandez had darker hair than the woman on the passport.

☐ b. the woman on the passport was larger and had longer hair and bigger lips.

☐ c. Fernandez was taller and younger than the woman pictured on the passport.

3. Which paragraphs provide information that supports your answer to question 2?

☐ a. paragraphs 7 and 9

☐ b. paragraphs 8 and 11

☐ c. paragraphs 9 and 10

4. Fernandez really wanted to escape from Cuba. What was one cause of her feelings?

☐ a. Fernandez wanted her daughter to have a better life.

☐ b. Fernandez wanted to be with her friend in Spain.

☐ c. Fernandez knew that the Cuban government was going to put her in jail if she stayed.

5. Which lesson about life does this story teach?

☐ a. You should always love your country.

☐ b. Always be honest.

☐ c. Never give up.

Score 4 points for each correct answer.

_____ **Total Score:** Critical Thinking

Enter your score for each activity. Add the scores together. Record your total score on the graph on page 115.

_____ Finding the Main Idea

_____ Recalling Facts

_____ Making Inferences

_____ Using Words

_____ Author's Approach

_____ Summarizing and Paraphrasing

_____ Critical Thinking

_____ **Total Score**

Personal Response

How do you think Fidel Castro felt when his daughter left Cuba?

_____

_____

Self-Assessment

One good question about this article that was not asked would be "_____

_____ ?"

Diving into Danger

Audrey Mestre is shown here smiling and waving after breaking her own free diving record in May 2001.

Audrey Mestre loved the ocean. As a child in France, she swam as much as she could. She would have liked to spend all her time in the water. And Mestre did not just swim. She also dived underwater. Her parents were scuba divers. They used air tanks to swim underwater. So it was natural for Mestre to dive. Growing up she spent summers at the sea. "I was diving every day," she said.

2   In college Mestre studied ocean life. She also studied what happens to people who make really deep dives. This kind of diving is called free diving or "no limits" diving. Free diving is simple. The divers take a deep breath. They hold it. Then they see how far down they can dive. They don't use air tanks. They use only their lungs.

3   Very few people do free diving. The sport takes great strength and daring. Free diving can be deadly. As a person goes deeper, water pressure builds. Everything inside the body gets squeezed. The lungs get as small as oranges. The heart slows down. It may beat fewer than 20 times a minute.

4   These changes in the body can cause big problems. Sometimes free divers black out. They go into a sleeplike state. They must be rescued quickly, or they will drown. So scuba divers keep watch on them. If a free diver gets into trouble, a scuba diver will move in to help.

5   Mestre decided to study a Cuban free diver named Pipin Ferreras. He held the world record. Ferreras could free dive 500 feet. In 1996 Mestre went to see him. She wanted to talk to him. She thought he might help with a paper she was writing. But something she didn't expect happened. She fell in love with him. Three years later they married.

6   Ferreras taught Mestre to free dive. She loved it. Free diving took her to "a magical world." To her the deep sea was "the only place to go and touch, feel, and live the power of the ocean." Soon Mestre dived as well as her husband. In fact, in some ways she dived better. Ferreras had a stronger body. But, as he said, "She has the stronger mind."

7   In 2002 Mestre tried to set a new record. She went down 558 feet. That broke the women's record. It even broke Ferreras's own mark. But because the record was set on a training dive, it didn't count. She would have to do the dive again, this time with judges present to write it down.

8   On October 12 Mestre got ready. There was no way she—or anyone—could free dive 500 feet using just arms and legs. So, like other free divers, she would hold onto a "sled" that weighs about 80 pounds. Mestre would ride the sled down. She would go as far as she wanted. Then she would inflate an air bag. That would

lift her and the sled back up. The whole dive would take about three minutes. That's a long time to go without air. But Mestre could do it. She had trained herself to hold her breath that long.

9   On the morning of the dive, a storm struck. Thunder roared, and lightning filled the sky. The wind blew hard. Ferreras wondered whether Mestre should postpone the dive. But then the weather calmed down. Mestre decided to go ahead. As Ferreras checked the equipment, Mestre slipped into her wet suit. Several scuba divers took up positions along the route. They would be there in case Mestre needed help. But she had made one thing clear. They were not to give her air unless she asked for it.

10   When Mestre was ready, she took a deep breath and began her dive. She raced down past the scuba divers. She reached the bottom of her dive in one minute and 42 seconds. That was faster than her practice dive. Now all she had to do was come up. But when Mestre tried to inflate the air bag, it didn't work. Something was wrong. The bag simply wouldn't inflate. And so the sled didn't rise.

11   The nearest scuba diver rushed to Mestre's side. He joined his air tank to her air bag. Air from the tank flowed into the bag. The sled began to rise, but not fast enough.

12   Mestre could have taken a breath from the scuba diver's air tank. But she didn't. She gave no sign that she wanted air. Taking a breath would have meant giving up her chance to set a record. Besides, it might have killed her. Mestre had never taken in air while so far down. It might have caused violent coughing. It might even have caused her lungs to explode.

13   As seconds passed, the sled slowly rose. The scuba diver struggled to push Mestre up. After nearly four minutes, Mestre blacked out. At last, she reached the top. But by then she had been underwater for more than eight minutes. Ferreras tried to pump air into her lungs. But it was no use. Audrey Mestre was dead.

14   Everyone felt awful. To honor Mestre, judges decided to count her practice dive. It was now a new record. No other human—male or female—had gone that deep.

15   After Mestre's death, some people called for a ban on free diving. They said that it was just too dangerous. But free diver Loic Leferme does not agree. He does not think free diving can be stopped. "It would be like trying to forbid people from climbing Everest," he said. "It's impossible."

A. Finding the Main Idea

One statement below tells the main idea of the article. One statement is too general, or too broad. The other statement explains only part of the article; it is too narrow. Label the statements using the following key:

M—Main Idea   B—Too Broad   N—Too Narrow

_____ 1. As a child, Audrey Mestre loved the sea. Her mother and father were scuba divers. When she grew up, she went to college and studied the ocean. She loved many water sports.

_____ 2. A daring woman named Audrey Mestre tried to break the free diving record. Something went wrong during the dive, and she died.

_____ 3. Some sports, such as free diving, take a lot of skill and strength. People who take up these sports must understand that they are putting their lives in danger.

Score 4 points for each correct answer.

_____ **Total Score:** Finding the Main Idea

B. Recalling Facts

How well do you remember the facts in the article? Put an X in the box next to the answer that correctly completes each statement.

1. Audrey Mestre grew up in

☐ a. France.
☐ b. the United States.
☐ c. Australia.

2. At first, Audrey Mestre wanted to meet Pipin Ferreras so that he would

☐ a. marry her.
☐ b. help her with a paper.
☐ c. help her set a free diving record.

3. Judges didn't want to count Mestre's 558-foot dive as a record because

☐ a. she was not a member of the Free Diving Club.
☐ b. nobody believed a woman could dive that deep.
☐ c. no officials saw her do it.

4. Mestre blacked out after being underwater for

☐ a. one minute and 42 seconds.
☐ b. nearly four minutes.
☐ c. eight minutes.

Score 4 points for each correct answer.

_____ **Total Score:** Recalling Facts

C. Making Inferences

When you draw a conclusion that is not directly stated in the text, you are making an inference. Put an X in the box next to the statement that is a correct inference.

1.

☐ a. Free diving is a good sport to do with no one else around.

☐ b. The scuba divers didn't try very hard to save Mestre's life.

☐ c. Mestre was probably a very good swimmer.

2.

☐ a. Mestre didn't know how the sled or the air bag worked.

☐ b. Some people really enjoy sports that put them in danger.

☐ c. Mestre didn't care much whether she made a free diving record or not.

Score 4 points for each correct answer.

_____ **Total Score:** Making Inferences

D. Using Words

Put an X in the box next to the definition below that is closest in meaning to the underlined word.

1. Let's get ready for the party. Your job is to inflate a balloon for each child who is coming.

☐ a. to make bigger by filling with air

☐ b. to make smaller by taking air away

☐ c. to walk or march in a parade

2. If it rains, we will postpone the picnic until a sunny day.

☐ a. decide never to do something again

☐ b. do something no matter how hard it is

☐ c. wait to do something until later

3. Her sneezes are so violent that people next door can hear them.

☐ a. very strong

☐ b. very soft

☐ c. very pretty

4. If you put too much air in the balloon, it will explode and wake the baby.

☐ a. fly away

☐ b. blow up

☐ c. cost too much

5. To keep the air clean, the mayor wants to put a <u>ban</u> on smoking in city hall.

☐ a. a right that people have

☐ b. a rule against something

☐ c. money collected for a special cause

6. Most parents <u>forbid</u> their children to stay out late on school nights.

☐ a. tell a joke or a funny story

☐ b. ask someone to do a favor

☐ c. order not to do something

Score 4 points for each correct answer.

_____ **Total Score:** Using Words

E Author's Approach

Put an X in the box next to the correct answer.

1. The author uses the first sentence of the article to

☐ a. tell one important thing about Audrey Mestre.

☐ b. describe free diving and why it is so dangerous.

☐ c. compare Audrey Mestre and her parents.

2. Choose the statement below that is the weakest argument for free diving.

☐ a. Free diving is fun.

☐ b. Free diving can take your life.

☐ c. Not many people are strong enough to free dive.

3. Choose the statement below that best describes the author's opinion in paragraph 12.

☐ a. Mestre did the right thing in not taking a breath from the tank, because doing that might have killed her.

☐ b. Mestre should have taken a breath from the scuba diver's air tank.

☐ c. Mestre was not thinking clearly when she was underwater.

Score 4 points for each correct answer.

_____ **Total Score:** Author's Approach

F. | Summarizing and Paraphrasing

Put an X in the box next to the correct answer.

1. Which summary says all the important things about the article?

☐ a. Free diving changes the body in many ways. Water pressure squeezes everything. The lungs shrink. The heart beats much slower.

☐ b. Before Audry Mestre made her last dive on October 12, 2002, a storm struck. Her husband thought she should put off making the dive. But when the weather got better, she decided to try it anyway.

☐ c. Free diver Audrey Mestre set a record in a training dive. On October 12, 2002, she lost her life while trying to repeat the dive for judges. She was given the record anyway.

2. Which sentence means the same thing as the following sentence? "Taking a breath would have meant giving up her chance to make a record."

☐ a. To make the record, she had to do the dive without taking a breath.

☐ b. If she took a breath, she would have had a chance to make the record.

☐ c. Even though she took a breath, she made the record.

> Score 4 points for each correct answer.
>
> _____ **Total Score:** Summarizing and Paraphrasing

G. | Critical Thinking

Put an X in the box next to the correct answer.

1. Choose the statement below that states an opinion.

☐ a. In a training dive, Mestre went down 558 feet.

☐ b. Mestre had trained herself to hold her breath about three minutes.

☐ c. No one should risk his or her life just to make a record.

2. Mestre and Ferreras were alike because

☐ a. both came from France.

☐ b. both were free divers.

☐ c. both made dives on October 12, 2002.

3. When Mestre was ready to go up after her dive, her air bag wouldn't inflate. What was the effect of that problem?

☐ a. The sled didn't rise.

☐ b. Mestre gave a sign that she wanted some air.

☐ c. Mestre started coughing and couldn't stop.

4. Which paragraph provides information that supports your answer to question 3?

☐ a. paragraph 2

☐ b. paragraph 10

☐ c. paragraph 13

5. If you were a free diver, how could you use the information in the article to make a record?

☐ a. I would practice holding my breath as long as I could.

☐ b. I would move to France to learn to swim well.

☐ c. Because the air bag caused trouble, I would not use an air bag. I would just pull the heavy sled up by myself.

Score 4 points for each correct answer.

_____ **Total Score:** Critical Thinking

Enter your score for each activity. Add the scores together. Record your total score on the graph on page 115.

_____ Finding the Main Idea

_____ Recalling Facts

_____ Making Inferences

_____ Using Words

_____ Author's Approach

_____ Summarizing and Paraphrasing

_____ Critical Thinking

_____ **Total Score**

Personal Response

I can't believe _____

_____

_____

Self-Assessment

From reading this article, I have learned _____

_____

_____

When Wild Animals Go Wild

Shown here is a Sumatran tiger similar to the one featured in this selection.

Hannah Goorsky had never worked in a zoo. But she loved animals. Goorsky was 23 years old. She was just out of college. She hoped one day to be an animal doctor. For now, though, she had some free time. She heard that the Sacramento Zoo needed volunteers. The volunteers would do work without getting paid. But they would learn more about the zoo. So she signed up.

2   Goorsky's parents were not surprised. Her mom said that Hannah had always loved spending time with animals. And she liked learning about them too.

3   The zoo housed wild animals. So Goorsky knew the work would have some risks. But she did not know just how dangerous it would turn out to be.

4   Goorsky's first day at the zoo was a quiet one. So was her second day. But the third day—March 23, 2003—was one she would never forget. It was a Sunday morning. Goorsky was still training and learning her way around the zoo. She went with zookeeper Chad Summers to the lions' den. She watched him feed the lions. Next he fed the snow leopard. Then Goorsky and Summers moved on to the tigers' den. This was where the Sumatran tigers lived.

5   The zoo had two Sumatran tigers. Castro was the male. Bahagia was the female. Sumatran tigers are the smallest of the world's tigers. But that does not mean they are tiny. A grown male is eight feet long. It may weigh 250 pounds or more. Castro was very big. He weighed 325 pounds.

6   Sumatran tigers are almost extinct. There are just 500 of them left in the wild. These tigers can be found in Asia. They live in the jungles of Sumatra in Indonesia. Another 250 or so live in zoos. Most of these are in Europe. So the Sacramento Zoo was lucky to have two.

7   Castro and Bahagia were beautiful. They had smooth orange coats with thin black stripes. But they also had strong jaws, big teeth, and sharp claws. They could pounce and kill in a flash. So the keepers took great care when dealing with these animals.

8   Summers made sure Castro and Bahagia were safely in the holding pen. This was a cage that kept the tigers out of the main den. Then Summers mixed the tigers' food, and Goorsky began to clean the den.

9   Summers set the food out. Castro started to eat. Then Summers saw that the cage door had not been fully closed. He rushed to close it. But he was not fast enough. Castro got his head and shoulders out the door. He bit Summers on his lower leg. He pulled Summers to the ground and bit him again.

10   Goorsky saw it happen. She knew she had to act fast. "There are always two kinds of girls in the movies," she

later said. There are "the ones who stand there screaming" when a bad guy attacks. And there are "the ones who grab a frying pan and bash him on the head."

11   She chose to be like the second kind. She grabbed a shovel. She swung it at the tiger. Again and again she hit him on the head. At last, Castro let go of Summers. The tiger moved back into the cage. Goorsky slammed the door shut. Summers had tiger bites on his neck. He had bites on his shoulder and leg too. But thanks to Goorsky, he was alive.

12   One zoo worker rushed to call 911. Others ran to give Summers first aid. They did their best to stop the bleeding. Soon a rescue squad arrived. They took the 30-year-old Summers to the hospital.

13   Everyone at the zoo said that Summers barely escaped. If not for Goorsky's quick response, Summers would be dead. Mary Healy, the head of the zoo, felt very lucky that Goorsky had been there to help.

14   That July, the City Council met with Goorsky. They honored her for what she had done. The mayor called Goorsky a hero. He also said, "It should be enough that you were volunteering at the zoo. But you've gone beyond that and also saved a life."

15   It took a while, but Summers's wounds did heal. Four months later, he was back at work. By then Goorsky was no longer there. She had taken a break from the zoo. But her love for animals was as strong as ever. She had found a job working for an animal doctor. And she said that in time she would go back to the zoo.

16   Both she and Summers had learned the hard way just how dangerous zoo work can be. Attacks are rare. But they do happen. This should not shock us. "These are still wild animals," said one zoo worker. Said another, "The first thing I tell people is a wild animal is like a loaded gun. It can go off at any time. This is the kind of business we are in."

A. Finding the Main Idea

One statement below tells the main idea of the article. One statement is too general, or too broad. The other statement explains only part of the article; it is too narrow. Label the statements using the following key:

M—Main Idea   B—Too Broad   N—Too Narrow

_____ 1. It is hard to guess what wild animals will do next. People around wild animals should be ready for anything all the time.

_____ 2. The Sacramento Zoo was lucky to have two rare Sumatran tigers. Most Sumatran tigers live in Asia. They have smooth orange coats and thin black stripes.

_____ 3. After a tiger attacked a zookeeper, a volunteer's quick work saved his life. What happened should remind us that wild animals can and do hurt people.

Score 4 points for each correct answer.

_____ **Total Score:** Finding the Main Idea

B. Recalling Facts

How well do you remember the facts in the article? Put an X in the box next to the answer that correctly completes each statement.

1. Hannah Goorsky planned on becoming
   - ☐ a. a zookeeper.
   - ☐ b. an animal doctor.
   - ☐ c. a college teacher.

2. About 500 Sumatran tigers live in
   - ☐ a. zoos in the United States.
   - ☐ b. zoos around the world.
   - ☐ c. the jungles of Asia.

3. The holding pen is a cage where
   - ☐ a. tigers stay when their main den is being cleaned.
   - ☐ b. people get a chance to touch or pet a tiger.
   - ☐ c. people who want to see tigers up close can stand.

4. Goorsky hit Castro with a
   - ☐ a. broom.
   - ☐ b. frying pan.
   - ☐ c. shovel.

Score 4 points for each correct answer.

_____ **Total Score:** Recalling Facts

C. Making Inferences

When you draw a conclusion that is not directly stated in the text, you are making an inference. Put an X in the box next to the statement that is a correct inference.

1.

☐ a. Sumatran tigers are the only dangerous animals at the zoo.

☐ b. It is not very important to be careful around wild animals, such as Sumatran tigers.

☐ c. Goorsky is a good person to have around when things go wrong.

2.

☐ a. Castro didn't even notice that Goorsky was hitting him on the head.

☐ b. Chad Summers is probably very happy that Hannah Goorsky was with him on the day Castro attacked.

☐ c. Seeing what the tiger did to Summers made Goorsky afraid of all animals.

Score 4 points for each correct answer.

_____ **Total Score:** Making Inferences

D. Using Words

Put an X in the box next to the definition below that is closest in meaning to the underlined word.

1. Instead of money, the club gave the <u>volunteers</u> a big party at the end of the year.

☐ a. people who won't work unless they are paid

☐ b. people who do work for free

☐ c. people who try to hurt others

2. If an animal becomes <u>extinct</u>, people will never see it again.

☐ a. scary

☐ b. died out

☐ c. very big

3. The cat waited outside the mouse hole so it could <u>pounce</u> on a mouse if it came out.

☐ a. jump to attack something

☐ b. sleep lightly or take a nap

☐ c. drink water from a bowl

4. Our next-door neighbor is the head of a police <u>squad</u> that handles problems in our neighborhood.

☐ a. an ocean animal that has ten arms

☐ b. a list of people who were just married

☐ c. a group of people who work together

5. As always, the fans' <u>response</u> to winning the game was cheers and shouts of joy.

☐ a. something that has never been done before
☐ b. something done as an answer
☐ c. anything that does not cost too much

6. Even after your cuts <u>heal</u>, you will still have scars.

☐ a. come back to good health
☐ b. start bleeding again
☐ c. begin to hurt again

Score 4 points for each correct answer.

_____ **Total Score:** Using Words

E. Author's Approach

Put an X in the box next to the correct answer.

1. The main purpose of the first paragraph is to

☐ a. describe the jobs Goorsky did as a zoo volunteer.
☐ b. explain how Goorsky came to be helping at the zoo.
☐ c. tell how dangerous wild animals can be.

2. Choose the statement below that best describes the author's opinion in paragraph 11.

☐ a. Chad Summers has Goorsky to thank for his life.
☐ b. Hannah Goorsky is not like the girls in the movies.
☐ c. Castro was meaner and stronger than other Sumatran tigers.

3. The author tells this story mainly by

☐ a. telling what happened in time order.
☐ b. comparing different ideas.
☐ c. using his or her imagination.

Score 4 points for each correct answer.

_____ **Total Score:** Author's Approach

F. Summarizing and Paraphrasing

Put an X in the box next to the correct answer.

1. Which summary says all the important things about the article?

   ☐ a. In 2003 Hannah Goorsky, a volunteer at Sacramento Zoo, saved the life of zookeeper Chad Summers. A tiger was attacking him. She beat the tiger back into its cage. Goorsky was honored as a hero.

   ☐ b. Hannah Goorsky loved working with animals. As a volunteer, she helped clean animal cages and dens. Soon after she got out of college, she started working for an animal doctor.

   ☐ c. The Sumatran tiger may someday become extinct. There are only about 750 Sumatran tigers left in the world. In 2003, one attacked a Sacramento zookeeper.

2. Which sentence means the same thing as the following sentence? "If not for Goorsky's quick response, Summers would be dead."

   ☐ a. Goorsky quickly answered that Summers would soon be dead.

   ☐ b. Summers would have died if Goorsky had acted fast.

   ☐ c. Summers would be dead now if Goorsky hadn't acted so quickly.

Score 4 points for each correct answer.

_____ **Total Score:** Summarizing and Paraphrasing

G. Critical Thinking

Put an X in the box next to the correct answer.

1. Choose the statement below that states a fact.

   ☐ a. Hannah Goorsky was braver than any other volunteer.

   ☐ b. Castro and Bahagia were rare Sumatran tigers.

   ☐ c. Sumatran tigers are too dangerous to be kept anywhere around people.

2. From information in the article, you can predict that

   ☐ a. from now on, the Sacramento Zoo will not use any volunteers.

   ☐ b. Goorsky will decide not to become an animal doctor.

   ☐ c. zookeeper Summers will be sure the tigers' cage door is closed the next time he feeds them.

3. Castro and Bahagia are different because

   ☐ a. only Castro attacked Summers.

   ☐ b. only Castro was put into the holding pen.

   ☐ c. only Castro had strong jaws, big teeth, and sharp claws.

4. Which paragraph provides information that supports your answer to question 3?

   ☐ a. paragraph 8

   ☐ b. paragraph 9

   ☐ c. paragraph 7

5. What was the effect of Castro's cage door's being left a little open?

☐ a. Goorsky was able to take a break from her zoo work and get a job with an animal doctor.

☐ b. Goorsky was able to clean the tigers' den.

☐ c. Castro was able to get his head and shoulders out the door.

Score 4 points for each correct answer.

_____ **Total Score:** Critical Thinking

Enter your score for each activity. Add the scores together. Record your total score on the graph on page 115.

_____ Finding the Main Idea

_____ Recalling Facts

_____ Making Inferences

_____ Using Words

_____ Author's Approach

_____ Summarizing and Paraphrasing

_____ Critical Thinking

_____ **Total Score**

Personal Response

I agree with the author because _____

_____

_____

Self-Assessment

Before reading this article, I already knew _____

_____

A Daring Rescue

Beck Weathers arrives in Katmandu, Nepal, after being rescued from Mount Everest during a mountain-climbing trip.

No one had ever flown a helicopter that far up Mount Everest. But someone had to try. If not, a climber would die. Several pilots were asked to do it. They said no. But one man said yes. His name was Madan K. C. He was a pilot in the Nepal Air Force. And he was ready to risk his life to help a stranded climber.

2   K. C. got the call on May 11, 1996. He was asked to rescue a man named Beck Weathers. Weathers was in a base camp at 20,000 feet. A day earlier, Weathers had been even higher. He had been near the 29,028-foot summit. That is the highest spot on Earth. But Weathers's eyes could not stand the high altitude. He had become nearly blind. So he had sat down to wait while Rob Hall, the group's leader, took others to the top. But Hall never came back. A big storm moved in. Hall and a few others were trapped near the summit. Eight of them died that night.

3   Weathers, too, almost died. The snow and wind blew all around him. The temperature dropped to 35 degrees below zero. For 14 hours he lay in the snow, barely breathing. Ice covered his face. But he wasn't ready to die. He thought about his wife and children. That gave him new strength. Somehow he picked himself up. He started walking. At 5 P.M. the next afternoon, he stumbled into one of the base camps.

4   No one there could believe it. They had thought for sure he was dead. They had even called his wife to tell her the bad news. Almost no one lives through a night on Mount Everest. Weathers himself didn't expect to get through it.

5   The climbers carried Weathers down to a lower camp. His arm was frozen. Much of his face was black with frostbite. And he still could not see. There was no way he could walk down the rest of the mountain. And it was too steep and icy for others to carry him any further. His only hope was to be flown out.

6   That's where Madan K. C. came in. K. C.'s mission was to fly to the base camp at 20,000 feet. To get there, K. C. would have to fly over a 22,000-foot ridge. He would land on a small patch of snow. He would pick up Weathers. Then he would fly out again.

7   The risks were huge. First, his helicopter was built to fly to only 20,000 feet. He would have to take it higher. Next, he might face high winds and blowing snow. And then there was the landing. K. C. had to land in just the right spot. Otherwise, the helicopter would crash.

8   K. C. knew the dangers he faced. Still, he got ready to go. He waited for the wind to calm down. Then he took off. Somehow he made it over the ridge. The climbers at the base camp had marked the landing spot with an X.

They had used a soft drink to color the snow. K. C. saw the spot and flew toward it.

9   Lying in the base camp, Weathers did not have much hope. He felt the chance of a rescue by air was "zero." Even as K. C. drew near, Weathers was not hopeful. "I didn't think he'd ever land," Weathers said. It just seemed too dangerous. As Weathers said, K. C. "had zero room for error."

10   Climber Ed Veisturs thought the same thing. He saw K. C. come in and circle. "We thought he was going to give up," said Veisturs. But K. C. circled around again. He landed perfectly. Weathers said it was "like a feather settling on the snow."

11   Weathers was thrilled. But then he thought of Makalu Gau. Gau was a climber from Taiwan. Gau, too, had had trouble near the top of the mountain. Like Weathers, he had lived through the night. He was at the base camp now too. And he was doing even worse. K. C. had come to rescue Weathers. But he could only fly out one climber at a time, so Weathers told him to take Gau. "It seemed like the thing to do at the time,"

Weathers later said. As soon as K. C. lifted off, Weathers lost hope. "I didn't think he was coming back," he said.

12   But Madan K. C. did come back. Once more he flew up over the ridge. Once more he made the tricky landing on the X. This time Weathers got in. And K. C. flew him safely down the mountain.

13   Both Gau and Weathers lived. Gau lost his arms, feet, and nose to frostbite. Weathers lost his nose, much of his right arm, and his left fingers. But his sight came back. And both he and Gau were grateful just to be alive.

14   K. C. was later asked if he had had any fear during the rescue mission. He said no. He had a job to do, and he did it. But then he said, "I am more fearful about it now that I think about it."

15   As for Beck Weathers, he said he would never climb Everest again. "The only way I'd go back to see the mountain is from the seat of a helicopter," he said. And if he did that, he would want Madan K. C. to be his pilot. "That's a guy with a big heart," said Weathers.

A. Finding the Main Idea

One statement below tells the main idea of the article. One statement is too general, or too broad. The other statement explains only part of the article; it is too narrow. Label the statements using the following key:

M—Main Idea   B—Too Broad   N—Too Narrow

_____ 1. Two men were hurt while climbing Mount Everest. A brave helicopter pilot faced danger and rescued them. The men survived.

_____ 2. Not everyone can climb Mount Everest. Only the best climbers make it to the top. It is easy to get hurt or get sick on the way up or down.

_____ 3. Beck Weathers became nearly blind as he climbed Mount Everest. He sat down to wait for other climbers to come back to him. But they were having their own troubles higher up the mountain.

Score 4 points for each correct answer.

_____ **Total Score:** Finding the Main Idea

B. Recalling Facts

How well do you remember the facts in the article? Put an X in the box next to the answer that correctly completes each statement.

1. On May 10, 1996, Beck Weathers stopped climbing to the top of Mount Everest because

☐ a. the thin air made him too tired to go all the way.

☐ b. the altitude made him nearly blind.

☐ c. his legs were covered with frostbite.

2. K. C.'s flight was risky because

☐ a. the helicopter was not built to fly that high.

☐ b. K. C. was not a very good pilot.

☐ c. K. C. did not know exactly where Weathers was waiting for him.

3. The first person that K. C. flew down the mountain was

☐ a. Beck Weathers.

☐ b. Ron Hall.

☐ c. Makalu Gau.

4. Weathers lived, but he lost his

☐ a. nose, part of his right arm, and his left fingers.

☐ b. arms, feet, and nose.

☐ c. right foot, left hand, and ears.

Score 4 points for each correct answer.

_____ **Total Score:** Recalling Facts

C. Making Inferences

When you draw a conclusion that is not directly stated in the text, you are making an inference. Put an X in the box next to the statement that is a correct inference.

1.

☐ a. Weathers knew that his wife and children needed him.

☐ b. Even though he was nearly blind, Weathers found it easy to walk down Mount Everest to the base camp.

☐ c. It would have been simple for K. C. to fly up and save the climbers trapped even higher up Mount Everest.

2.

☐ a. Weathers was selfish and thought only of his own safety.

☐ b. The blowing snow made it impossible for K. C. to see where he should land the helicopter.

☐ c. K. C. was a good pilot as well as a brave and kind man.

> Score 4 points for each correct answer.
>
> _____ **Total Score:** Making Inferences

D. Using Words

Put an X in the box next to the definition below that is closest in meaning to the underlined word.

1. The unhappy stranded sailors sat on the beach. They hoped a ship would come by and save them.

☐ a. not able to make friends

☐ b. left somewhere feeling helpless

☐ c. excited and joyful

2. The man pulled himself up to the summit of the mountain and looked at the valley below.

☐ a. highest point

☐ b. lowest point

☐ c. cold, dark cave

3. At a high altitude, the air is thin. That is why some people who climb tall mountains feel sick.

☐ a. distance above the level of the sea

☐ b. distance between big cities

☐ c. distance between people climbing a mountain

4. Cover up your ears and fingers when you ski, or you might get frostbite.

☐ a. a feeling of being lost or puzzled

☐ b. a prize for doing something special

☐ c. harm done to body parts by the cold

5. Your secret <u>mission</u> is to find out the name of the spy.

☐ a. place
☐ b. surprise
☐ c. job

6. Look up at the line of trees growing on that <u>ridge</u>.

☐ a. tall building in the middle of a city
☐ b. long, narrow top of a mountain
☐ c. rowboat or other small boat

Score 4 points for each correct answer.

_____ **Total Score:** Using Words

E. Author's Approach

Put an X in the box next to the correct answer.

1. What is the author's purpose in writing this article?

☐ a. to get the reader to climb Mount Everest
☐ b. to tell the reader about a rescue on Mount Everest
☐ c. to describe what happens when a person gets frostbite

2. From the statements below, choose the one that you believe the author would agree with.

☐ a. Weathers will probably change his mind and try to climb Mount Everest again.
☐ b. Gau wasn't really hurt as badly as Weathers.
☐ c. Gau owes his life to Weathers and K. C.

3. The author tells this story mainly by

☐ a. describing what happened in time order.
☐ b. comparing and contrasting different topics.
☐ c. using his or her imagination.

Score 4 points for each correct answer.

_____ **Total Score:** Author's Approach

F. Summarizing and Paraphrasing

Put an X in the box next to the correct answer.

1. Which summary says all the important things about the article?

☐ a. Beck Weathers almost died when he had to stay overnight near the top of Mount Everest. That night, the temperature dropped to 35 degrees below zero. He got frostbite that night.

☐ b. Madan K. C. was a pilot in the Nepal Air Force. He knew that his helicopter was built to fly to only 20,000 feet. He found out that it could go even higher.

☐ c. Beck Weathers nearly became blind when climbing Mount Everest. Helicopter pilot Madan K. C. flew up to get him, even though the flight was risky. K. C. saved Weathers and another climber.

2. Which sentence means the same thing as the following sentence? "As Weathers said, K. C. 'had zero room for error.'"

☐ a. K. C. did not have much room in his helicopter.

☐ b. K. C. could not make any mistakes, or he would fail.

☐ c. K. C. had never made any mistakes in his life.

Score 4 points for each correct answer.

_____ **Total Score:** Summarizing and Paraphrasing

G. Critical Thinking

Put an X in the box next to the correct answer.

1. Choose the statement below that states a fact.

☐ a. Mount Everest is 29,028 feet tall.

☐ b. K. C. should not have tried to make his helicopter fly so high.

☐ c. It's not fair to ask anyone to risk his or her life for a stranger.

2. From information in the article, you can infer that

☐ a. none of the climbers on that trip will ever climb mountains again.

☐ b. Weathers and Gau thanked K. C. for saving them.

☐ c. a landing strip will be built at the summit of Mount Everest so no one will ever have to climb the mountain again.

3. Weathers and Gau are alike because they both

☐ a. began their climb up Mount Everest with Madan K. C.

☐ b. survived a night on Mount Everest.

☐ c. lost their feet to frostbite.

4. What was the cause of Weathers's frostbite?

☐ a. He was very tired and wanted to get off the mountain.

☐ b. His eyes could not stand the high altitude.

☐ c. He had been out in the cold for too long.

5. How is K. C.'s rescue flight an example of going into the danger zone?

☐ a. K. C. picked up Makalu Gau first. He did not have enough room for two people on the helicopter.

☐ b. K. C. landed his helicopter "like a feather settling on the snow."

☐ c. K. C.'s helicopter could have crashed, and he might have died.

Score 4 points for each correct answer.

_____ **Total Score:** Critical Thinking

Enter your score for each activity. Add the scores together. Record your total score on the graph on page 115.

_____ Finding the Main Idea

_____ Recalling Facts

_____ Making Inferences

_____ Using Words

_____ Author's Approach

_____ Summarizing and Paraphrasing

_____ Critical Thinking

_____ **Total Score**

Personal Response

A question I would like K. C. to answer is "_____

_____

_____ ?"

Self-Assessment

One of the things I did best when reading this article was

_____

_____

I believe I did this well because _____

_____

_____

Compare and Contrast

Pick two stories in Unit One that tell about someone who stepped into the danger zone.
Use information from the stories to fill in this chart.

Title	Who was this person?	What did that person do?	What was the result?

Write the headline for a newspaper article about one of these stories. _____

_____

UNIT TWO

Risky Rescue

On September 11, 1999, a tugboat named *Gulf Majesty* left Florida. Its job was to pull a barge to Puerto Rico. A barge is a boat with a flat bottom. It carries goods from one place to another. This was not a good time for the boats to leave port. Everyone knew a big storm was coming. But the owners of the tug thought their crew could stay ahead of the bad weather. They were wrong. Hurricane Floyd moved in and caught *Gulf Majesty.* "We were trying to outrun it," said crew member Kim Brooks, "but it was faster than we were."

2   By the night of September 14, waves and winds were battering the tugboat. The next morning, things were even worse. Crew member Gerald Keeth had never seen seas so rough. Waves 40 feet high hit the tug. The waves almost pushed the tug over onto its side. Under such pounding, the tug began to sink. Captain John Dalton knew what he had to do. He told his seven crew members to cut the barge loose. They were going to leave the boat behind.

Shown here are crew members from the tugboat Gulf Majesty *arriving on the aircraft carrier* John F. Kennedy *after being rescued at sea.*

3   The *Gulf Majesty* had one raft. Five of the crew climbed into it. But before the other three could do the same, the lines holding the raft to the tug snapped. In the rough seas, the raft quickly drifted away. It happened so fast that there was nothing the men on the tug could do. "It was like watching hope float away," said Keeth. "To be honest, I was scared to death."

4   The three men had no choice. If they stayed on the tug, they would go down with it. So David Lytle, Tim Chambers, and Keeth put on their life jackets. Then, just 15 minutes before the tug sank, they jumped into the water.

5   In an effort to stay together, they held onto a long stick. They tried to kick and paddle to the raft 300 yards away. But it was no use. The sea was much too wild. So they stopped trying. They knew they had to conserve their energy.

6   The captain had sent a distress signal before leaving the tug. And Keeth had a locator beacon on him. It would send out a signal that rescue workers might pick up. So there was hope that the men might be found. They just had to stay calm and wait.

7   "We're going to make it," they told one another. "There's no problem." But in their hearts, they worried that rescue workers would not come. Said Keeth, "There was a number of times I doubted they would find us."

8 Luckily, help was not too far away. A Navy aircraft carrier, USS *John F. Kennedy,* was in the region. An aircraft carrier is a large ship that holds airplanes and helicopters. The *Kennedy* was just 150 miles from the *Gulf Majesty.* Men on the *Kennedy* heard the tug's distress signal. They rushed to help. They sent two helicopters off in search of the tug's crew.

9 It took the rescue workers a while to find the three men in the water. At last they did. By then these men had been adrift in the sea for close to four hours. They were thrilled to see the helicopters arrive. "That was a beautiful sight," said Keeth. "We weren't really looking at helicopters. We were looking at angels coming."

10 Shad Hernandez was one of the rescue workers. Hernandez had been trained to rescue people from the water. He had done it many times in practice. But it had always been in calm waters. Now he faced the toughest test of his life.

11 "I was scared," Hernandez admitted. "I didn't know what was going to happen."

12 The others on the helicopter were scared too. They had never done a rescue in waters so rough.

13 "Are you sure you're ready to go into that water?" the pilot asked Hernandez several times.

14 Hernandez knew the risks. But this was his job. It was what he was trained to do. It was also the only way to save the men in the water below.

15 "Yes, sir!" Hernandez said.

16 The pilot tried to hold the helicopter steady.

Hernandez slid down a rope. He dropped into the rough water. Then he fought his way through waves to the men 30 yards away. One by one, he hooked each man to a rescue harness. Then they were lifted out of the sea. They were pulled into the helicopter. When the last man was being brought up, Hernandez grabbed the rope and came up with him.

17 "I was in the water only 11 minutes," Hernandez said.

18 The helicopters went back to the aircraft carrier to get more fuel. Then they went looking for the bright orange raft. By the time they found it, the five men on it had been out on the sea for eight hours. Kim Brooks was in great pain. He had hurt his back when a monster wave nearly bent the raft in half. "I thought it was the end," he said. "It just kept getting rougher and rougher."

19 But again there were heroes on the scene. One of the two rescue swimmers was Shawn Whitfield. Like Hernandez, he was scared. For a while, he even felt sick. But then he saw the men alive, and "everything cleared again."

20 The five men were quickly lifted from the raft. They were whisked back to join their three mates on the carrier.

21 Gerald Keeth had high praise for all the rescue workers. "You wonder what your life is worth," he said. "And then someone really shows you—it's worth *their* life. That's the biggest price anyone can pay."

A. Finding the Main Idea

One statement below tells the main idea of the article. One statement is too general, or too broad. The other statement explains only part of the article; it is too narrow. Label the statements using the following key:

M—Main Idea   B—Too Broad   N—Too Narrow

_____ 1. True courage does not mean that you feel no fear. It means doing what you should in spite of your fears.

_____ 2. A storm with 40-foot waves hit the tugboat *Gulf Majesty* on its way to Puerto Rico. The captain ordered the crew to leave the ship behind. Five men got on a raft, and three were left behind.

_____ 3. Members of a tugboat crew who had abandoned ship were drifting in a rough sea. Trained swimmers were able to rescue them by pulling them into a helicopter.

Score 4 points for each correct answer.

_____ **Total Score:** Finding the Main Idea

B. Recalling Facts

How well do you remember the facts in the article? Put an X in the box next to the answer that correctly completes each statement.

1. The storm that hit the *Gulf Majesty* was
   - ☐ a. Hurricane Floyd.
   - ☐ b. a tornado.
   - ☐ c. a terrible snowstorm.

2. To stay together, three members of the crew
   - ☐ a. held hands.
   - ☐ b. held onto a long stick.
   - ☐ c. held onto a long rope.

3. Rescue worker Shad Hernandez was nervous because
   - ☐ a. he had not been trained to rescue people from the water.
   - ☐ b. even though he had been trained well, this water was rougher than he liked.
   - ☐ c. he was not a strong swimmer and was afraid that he was going to look silly.

4. The rescue workers were able to find the raft because
   - ☐ a. the captain had sent out a distress signal.
   - ☐ b. one of the men on the raft had a cell phone with him.
   - ☐ c. it was colored bright orange.

Score 4 points for each correct answer.

_____ **Total Score:** Recalling Facts

C. Making Inferences

When you draw a conclusion that is not directly stated in the text, you are making an inference. Put an X in the box next to the statement that is a correct inference.

1.

☐ a. The three men who floated in the water for four hours probably would have survived even without wearing life jackets.

☐ b. The crew of the USS *John F. Kennedy* took the *Gulf Majesty*'s distress signal very seriously.

☐ c. If the crew of the *Gulf Majesty* had been more careful, the lines holding the raft to the tug would not have snapped.

2.

☐ a. By staying with Keeth, the two other men in the water helped their chances of being rescued.

☐ b. Hernandez would have done a better job if he had stayed in the water longer than 11 minutes.

☐ c. The rescue workers took hours to rescue the men in the raft because they didn't really care about them.

Score 4 points for each correct answer.

_____ **Total Score:** Making Inferences

D. Using Words

Put an X in the box next to the definition below that is closest in meaning to the underlined word.

1. Waves had been <u>battering</u> the rock for years and slowly wearing it away.

☐ a. pounding against
☐ b. flowing away from
☐ c. drying up

2. We must <u>conserve</u> our money, or we will run out of it.

☐ a. enjoy
☐ b. spend
☐ c. save

3. The driver with a flat tire waved a white cloth to show that she and her car were in <u>distress</u>.

☐ a. a state of being ready
☐ b. a state of being curious
☐ c. a state of being in trouble

4. This <u>region</u> of the country is famous for its high mountains.

☐ a. name
☐ b. area
☐ c. leader

5. The boat couldn't get its engines going. It was <u>adrift</u> for several hours before another boat towed it to shore.

☐ a. floating freely
☐ b. running well
☐ c. taking on passengers

6. The woman dreamed of being <u>whisked</u> to a warm, sunny island.

☐ a. recorded
☐ b. carried quickly
☐ c. sung in a loud voice

Score 4 points for each correct answer.

_____ **Total Score:** Using Words

E. Author's Approach

Put an X in the box next to the correct answer.

1. The author uses the first sentence of the article to

☐ a. tell when and where the story takes place.
☐ b. describe what happens when a boat is caught in a hurricane.
☐ c. compare tugboats and barges.

2. The author probably wrote this article in order to

☐ a. get people to wear locator beacons when they go into dangerous places.
☐ b. explain what causes a hurricane.
☐ c. tell how brave people helped others in need.

3. The author tells this story mainly by

☐ a. describing events in time order.
☐ b. comparing different topics.
☐ c. using his or her imagination.

Score 4 points for each correct answer.

_____ **Total Score:** Author's Approach

F. Summarizing and Paraphrasing

Put an X in the box next to the correct answer.

1. Which summary says all the important things about the article?

☐ a. Even though they knew a storm was coming, the crew of the *Gulf Majesty* set out on September 11, 1999. By September 14, the tugboat had started to sink.

☐ b. Shad Hernandez faced danger off the coast of Florida. He and swimmer Shawn Whitfield overcame their fears to rescue people drifting in the sea.

☐ c. Caught in Hurricane Floyd, the crew of *Gulf Majesty* had to leave the ship behind. Five crew members were able to get into a raft, and three had to jump into the rough water. Brave rescue workers saved them by pulling them into helicopters.

2. Which sentence means the same thing as the following sentence? "He had hurt his back when a monster wave nearly bent the raft in half."

☐ a. Brooks hurt his back when he tried to bend the raft in half after it was hit by a wave.

☐ b. The raft was hurt by a big wave that nearly bent Brooks in half.

☐ c. A really big wave hit the raft hard and hurt Brooks's back.

Score 4 points for each correct answer.

_____ **Total Score:** Summarizing and Paraphrasing

G. Critical Thinking

Put an X in the box next to the correct answer.

1. Choose the statement below that states a fact.

☐ a. The safety of the crew of the *Gulf Majesty* was more important than the safety of the rescue workers.

☐ b. Some of the waves that hit the *Gulf Majesty* were about 40 feet high.

☐ c. The swimmers should have waited until the weather cleared up to save the crew of the *Gulf Majesty*.

2. Shad Hernandez and Shawn Whitfield are alike because

☐ a. both drifted in the raft for about eight hours.

☐ b. both were members of the crew of the *Gulf Majesty*.

☐ c. both were afraid of the rough water.

3. What was the cause of the three crew members' decision to jump off the tugboat into the water?

☐ a. They didn't want to go down with the tugboat.

☐ b. They wanted to try to swim to the *Kennedy*.

☐ c. They were angry with the crew members in the raft and wanted to swim away from them.

4. How are the rescue workers examples of people willing to go into the danger zone?

☐ a. It took hours to find the crew of the *Gulf Majesty*.

☐ b. They might have been hurt or drowned, yet they went ahead anyway.

☐ c. They did not waste any time getting to where they were needed.

5. If you were a tugboat captain, how could you use the information in the article to make sure you made money and kept your boat safe?

☐ a. I would not take the boat out when a bad storm was due.

☐ b. If I knew a bad storm was coming, I would try to go faster than it.

☐ c. I would not pull a barge from Florida to Puerto Rico.

Score 4 points for each correct answer.

_____ **Total Score:** Critical Thinking

Enter your score for each activity. Add the scores together. Record your total score on the graph on page 115.

_____ Finding the Main Idea

_____ Recalling Facts

_____ Making Inferences

_____ Using Words

_____ Author's Approach

_____ Summarizing and Paraphrasing

_____ Critical Thinking

_____ **Total Score**

Personal Response

Why do you think the helicopter pilot asked Hernandez several times whether he was ready to go into the water?

_____

_____

Self-Assessment

A word or phrase in the article that I do not understand is

_____

_____

Feel the Thrill

Marta Empinotti doesn't think of herself as an outlaw. But she is. What she does is against the law. If she gets caught, she might get off with just a warning. Or she might have to pay a fine. Empinotti might even go to jail. But that doesn't stop her. She has broken the law hundreds of times. And it makes her happy.

2   To be clear, it isn't breaking the law that puts a smile on her face. It is her extreme sport. Empinotti is a BASE jumper, and BASE jumping is illegal. The name of the sport comes from the objects people jump from. The *B* stands for buildings. The *A* is for antennas, another name for towers. The *S* is for spans, or bridges. The *E* stands for earth, usually cliffs. Empinotti has jumped off all four of these fixed objects. But in most places, such jumps are against the law. "I don't jump because I like to do something illegal," she says. "I jump because this is my love. . . . I jump because of the joy it gives me."

3   This is not a sport for everyone. There are only a few hundred BASE jumpers in the world. The reason for the

Shown here is a man jumping off Angel Falls in Venezuela. He is practicing BASE jumping, which is the subject of this selection.

small number is simple. Many BASE jumpers die. In the first 20 years of BASE jumping as a sport, 39 jumpers died. In large part, this is because they begin their jumps so close to the ground. They use parachutes, but they have only a few seconds to open them. Skydivers jump from planes high in the sky. If the main chute doesn't open, there is time to open a second chute. BASE jumpers often jump from less than 1,000 feet. If their main chute doesn't open, there's little time for a second chute.

4   Empinotti was born in Brazil. As a teenager she took up skydiving. She liked the feeling of freedom it gave her. Later, she left home to travel the world. By 1986 she was in Florida. One day a friend told her about Bridge Day. It is held every October in West Virginia. Bridge Day is a rare BASE jumping event. It is not against the law. Jumpers go off the bridge over the New River Gorge. Empinotti jumped and fell in love with BASE jumping.

5   She soon gave up skydiving. There were things about it that she did not like. She didn't like the noise of the plane. She didn't like the blast of wind caused by the engines. BASE jumping is silent. "There is no noise when you exit and no air speed," she says. "You start going faster and begin to hear the whoosh. You see the object—the tower or cliff or building—speeding by and

the ground rushing up." Such a fall would fill most people with terror. That is not true for Empinotti. "It fills me with life," she says.

6   Even the death of her boyfriend didn't stop her. In 1987 Empinotti and Steve Gyrsting went to Bridge Day. The bridge is 876 feet above the river. Steve jumped first. When his main parachute didn't open, he pulled the cord on his second chute, but it was too late. He was going too fast. With such a short jump, there was no time. Steve Gyrsting hit the water at more than 100 miles an hour.

7   Gyrsting's death troubled Empinotti. "For six months after that I just wanted to die," she admits. "I would climb up an object, think of him, start to cry, and climb back down."

8   But Empinotti loved BASE jumping too much to give it up forever. "I couldn't live without it," she says. "I would die inside." So in time she started jumping again. "It's still very sad for me," she declares. "I'll never get over it in a way. But I never feel guilty. . . . Steve made his own decision."

9   And so again Empinotti traveled the world in search of new jumps. Her sport took her to Norway. It took her to Germany and South Africa. She jumped off an office building in Venezuela. She also jumped the 3,200-foot Angel Falls in Venezuela.

10   Empinotti had some narrow escapes along the way. Once she was hit by lightning. One day the lines on her chute got twisted. Luckily, on that jump she was going off a cliff. She hit a small ledge before falling too far. That saved her life. Once she crashed into trees at the bottom of Angel Falls but survived.

11   Since BASE jumping is illegal, BASE jumpers have to be sneaky. They often get up before dawn. Then they slip into a building or up a tower. Sometimes they have to pick locks to get in. Other times they try to fool guards. They dress as if they are going to work in an office. They might carry what looks like a gift box. But inside the box are parachutes. The jumpers sneak onto the roof and wait for the building to close. "It brings out the James Bond in you," says one jumper. "It has to stay hush-hush."

12   One of Empinotti's favorite jumps is near her home. It is a 900-foot radio tower in central Florida. She jumps at dawn before anyone is around. Empinotti loves the tower. "Most people look at a tower as just a pile of steel," she says. "To me it is a thing of beauty."

13   Each time she reaches the top of the tower, she stops to enjoy the view. She watches the sun come up. "It's so peaceful. . . . It's just me and nature," Empinotti says. "Then I jump and feel the thrill."

A. | Finding the Main Idea

One statement below tells the main idea of the article. One statement is too general, or too broad. The other statement explains only part of the article; it is too narrow. Label the statements using the following key:

M—Main Idea   B—Too Broad   N—Too Narrow

_____ 1. Marta Empinotti was born in Brazil. She took up skydiving when she was a teenager. But she didn't like the noise the plane made. She didn't like the blast of wind the engines caused either.

_____ 2. Nothing can stop Marta Empinotti from her favorite sport, BASE jumping. Even though it is illegal and dangerous, she continues to jump all around the world.

_____ 3. It takes a certain kind of person to take up BASE jumping. It is a sport that is both dangerous and illegal. BASE jumpers risk their lives with each jump.

Score 4 points for each correct answer.

_____ **Total Score:** Finding the Main Idea

B. | Recalling Facts

How well do you remember the facts in the article? Put an X in the box next to the answer that correctly completes each statement.

1. The *B* in BASE jumping stands for
   - ☐ a. buildings.
   - ☐ b. branches.
   - ☐ c. balance.

2. Empinotti's boyfriend, Steve Gyrsting, died when he jumped from a
   - ☐ a. cliff.
   - ☐ b. bridge.
   - ☐ c. tower.

3. After her boyfriend's death, Empinotti couldn't jump for about
   - ☐ a. nine years.
   - ☐ b. six months.
   - ☐ c. three weeks.

4. When Empinotti's chute became twisted during a jump from a cliff, she saved her life by
   - ☐ a. opening a second chute and floating down to the ground.
   - ☐ b. falling into a group of trees at the bottom.
   - ☐ c. hitting a small ledge, which broke her fall.

Score 4 points for each correct answer.

_____ **Total Score:** Recalling Facts

59

C. Making Inferences

When you draw a conclusion that is not directly stated in the text, you are making an inference. Put an X in the box next to the statement that is a correct inference.

1.

☐ a. Empinotti is a strong person in good shape.

☐ b. BASE jumpers have great respect for the law.

☐ c. Skydiving is even more dangerous than BASE jumping.

2.

☐ a. BASE jumping is dangerous only if you are falling toward solid ground.

☐ b. BASE jumping off the New River Gorge Bridge in West Virginia is allowed all the time.

☐ c. Part of the fun of BASE jumping is the thrill that it can provide.

Score 4 points for each correct answer.

_____ **Total Score:** Making Inferences

D. Using Words

Put an X in the box next to the definition below that is closest in meaning to the underlined word.

1. The <u>outlaw</u> hid from the police in an empty building.

☐ a. a person who obeys the law

☐ b. one who writes the laws

☐ c. someone who breaks the law

2. Be sure to wear a helmet, because it is <u>illegal</u> to ride your bike without one.

☐ a. against the law

☐ b. a good idea

☐ c. allowed by the law

3. We could not move the park bench because it was <u>fixed</u> in cement.

☐ a. blowing in the wind

☐ b. held in place

☐ c. made of plastic

4. The child was afraid of spiders, so finding two of them in his lunch box filled him with <u>terror</u>.

☐ a. wonder

☐ b. happiness

☐ c. great fear

5. She feels <u>guilty</u> because she ate the last piece of pizza even though her friend wanted it.

☐ a.   bad for having done something wrong
☐ b.   proud of doing something right
☐ c.   tired after doing a hard job

6. Winning the award was a <u>thrill</u> I will never forget.

☐ a.   a feeling of sadness
☐ b.   a feeling of excitement
☐ c.   a feeling of being bored

Score 4 points for each correct answer.

_____ **Total Score:** Using Words

E. Author's Approach

Put an X in the box next to the correct answer.

1. The main purpose of the first paragraph is to

☐ a.   list all the ways that Marta Empinotti has been punished for BASE jumping in the United States.
☐ b.   describe what happens every time anyone BASE jumps.
☐ c.   explain that Marta Empinotti enjoys doing something that is against the law.

2. From the statements below, choose the one that you believe the author would agree with.

☐ a.   If BASE jumping were allowed by the law, Empinotti would give it up.
☐ b.   Steve Gyrsting didn't want to jump from the bridge over the New River Gorge.
☐ c.   BASE jumpers really love their sport.

3. The author probably wrote this article in order to

☐ a.   tell about a person who risks her life for fun.
☐ b.   get the reader to take up BASE jumping.
☐ c.   get governments to change the laws against BASE jumping.

Score 4 points for each correct answer.

_____ **Total Score:** Author's Approach

F. Summarizing and Paraphrasing

Put an X in the box next to the correct answer.

1. Which summary says all the important things about the article?

☐ a. BASE jumper Marta Empinotti enjoys her sport even though it is against the law and dangerous. Her boyfriend died in a jump. Even so, she still travels around the world finding good places to jump.

☐ b. Marta Empinotti lost a friend to the dangerous sport of BASE jumping. In 1987 Steve Gyrsting jumped off a bridge. His main chute didn't open.

☐ c. BASE jumpers have to be sneaky to take part in their sport. Sometimes, they sneak into a building. They wait until everyone has gone home to make their jump.

2. Which sentence means the same thing as the following sentence? "'It brings out the James Bond in you,' says one jumper."

☐ a. One jumper says that people who BASE jump should be put in jail.

☐ b. One jumper believes that sneaking around to BASE jump makes you feel like a spy.

☐ c. One jumper says he feels like an outlaw when he tries to have fun with his sport.

Score 4 points for each correct answer.

_____ **Total Score:** Summarizing and Paraphrasing

G. Critical Thinking

Put an X in the box next to the correct answer.

1. Choose the statement below that states a fact.

☐ a. BASE jumping is a wonderful sport.

☐ b. BASE jumping should be allowed by the law.

☐ c. Marta Empinotti was born in Brazil.

2. From information in the article, you can predict that

☐ a. Empinotti will soon see that BASE jumping is too dangerous for anyone to do.

☐ b. Empinotti will keep jumping as long as she can.

☐ c. soon, just about everyone will be BASE jumping.

3. BASE jumping and skydiving are different because

☐ a. BASE jumping is legal, but skydiving is illegal.

☐ b. skydivers usually have time to open a second chute if their first one fails.

☐ c. BASE jumping is dangerous, but skydiving isn't dangerous at all.

4. Steve Gyrsting's main parachute didn't open on a jump from a bridge. What was the effect of that?

☐ a. He hit the water going over 100 miles per hour.

☐ b. Empinotti travels all over the world looking for new places to jump.

☐ c. BASE jumping is illegal in most places around the world.

5. Which paragraph provides the information that supports your answer to question 4?

☐ a. paragraph 4

☐ b. paragraph 6

☐ c. paragraph 8

Score 4 points for each correct answer.

_____ **Total Score:** Critical Thinking

Enter your score for each activity. Add the scores together. Record your total score on the graph on page 115.

_____ Finding the Main Idea

_____ Recalling Facts

_____ Making Inferences

_____ Using Words

_____ Author's Approach

_____ Summarizing and Paraphrasing

_____ Critical Thinking

_____ **Total Score**

Personal Response

What new question do you have about this topic?

_____

_____

Self-Assessment

I can't really understand how _____

_____

_____

To the Top of the World

Erik Weihenmayer lost his sight when he was 13 years old. A rare disorder caused him to go blind. As his sight faded, Weihenmayer had to give up many of the sports he loved. He could no longer play basketball. He couldn't catch a football or ride a bike. But that didn't mean he sat around and did nothing. There were still plenty of things Weihenmayer could do. One of these things, it turned out, was mountain climbing.

2 Weihenmayer went rock climbing for the first time when he was 16. He loved it. When he climbed, it didn't matter so much that he was blind. He could hear the sound his ax made against rocks. The sound told him whether the rock was solid. His sense of touch told him where to place his hands and feet. And his sense of balance kept him from falling.

3 By the time he was 26, Weihenmayer had made a number of short climbs. He began to take on bigger mountains. First he climbed Denali, the highest peak in North America. Later, he climbed high mountains in Africa, South America, and Antarctica. Along the way, Weihenmayer learned many things. He learned to use

Erik Weihenmayer is shown near the top of Mount Everest.

walking poles. These helped him feel for deadly holes in the snow. He learned to listen for sounds of ice breaking or rocks shifting. And he learned to make a map of the mountain in his mind.

4 By 2001 Weihenmayer felt ready for the biggest challenge of all. He wanted to climb Mount Everest. Everest is the highest mountain in the world. Some people thought he was crazy. More than a hundred people have died on this mountain. Most were strong climbers, with all their senses intact. If they couldn't survive Everest, what chance did a blind man have?

5 But Weihenmayer thought differently. He believed he had the skills to make the climb. He was strong, and he was careful. And most importantly, he was tough, both in body and mind.

6 Weihenmayer put together a team of 10 men. In the spring of 2001, this group started up Everest. At first, Weihenmayer struggled. The team had to cross a big ice field littered with huge chunks of ice. There was no pattern for Weihenmayer to follow. Without a pattern, he could not predict what the next step would bring. Crossing that field was, said Weihenmayer, "a blind person's worst nightmare." The team had to make several trips over this ice field to get their gear to base camp. A good climber who can see might cross the field in seven hours. It took Weihenmayer 13 hours.

7   When Weihenmayer reached the other side, he was exhausted. His climbing partners told him to rest. They offered to make the rest of the trips across the ice field for him, but Weihenmayer refused. He did not want to be a burden to his fellow climbers. He wanted to be a full member of the team.

8   In all, Weihenmayer made 10 trips across the ice field. Each time he got better at it. By the last crossing, he had cut his time to just five hours.

9   By May 24 the team was near the top of the mountain. With one final push, they could make it to the summit. But a storm began. The wind blew, and snow and lightning filled the sky. If the storm didn't pass quickly, they would have to turn around and head down. "We thought we were done," Weihenmayer recalled.

10   Luckily, the storm did pass quickly. Weihenmayer and his climbing partners decided to keep going. But the weather was still harsh, and the climbing was difficult. As Weihenmayer said, "One wrong step could kill you." In some ways, though, Weihenmayer had an advantage. The men used oxygen masks to breathe. They also put on special glasses to protect their eyes. Wearing those, they could not see their feet. Some of the climbers found that hard. But Weihenmayer was used to climbing that way. In addition, much of the trip was made at night. The climbers had only their headlamps for light. Again, Weihenmayer had no trouble. He was used to climbing in darkness.

11   At last, on May 25, the group reached the summit. Erik Weihenmayer became the first blind person ever to stand on the top of Mount Everest. It was a great moment for him. It was a great moment for everyone else on his team too. He later said, "I get the praise for overcoming blindness. But everyone on the team overcame something to get there."

12   He was right. Jeff Evans defeated illness. Evans lost 30 pounds on the climb. But he made it. So did Eric Alexander. Alexander had been badly hurt on a mountain a year earlier. He beat his fears to make it to the top. And Brad Bull overcame worries about his age. At 64, Bull was the oldest person ever to scale Mount Everest.

13   Weihenmayer was pleased with his success. But he was not done yet. He went on to climb the highest peaks on the other continents. And he took up other tough sports. He found happiness even though he was blind. The secret, he said, was not to think about all the things he couldn't do but to focus on what he could do.

A. Finding the Main Idea

One statement below tells the main idea of the article. One statement is too general, or too broad. The other statement explains only part of the article; it is too narrow. Label the statements using the following key:

M—Main Idea   B—Too Broad   N—Too Narrow

_____ 1. Erik Weinhenmayer could not see, but he used other senses when climbing mountains. He listened for the sound his ax made against rocks. He felt around carefully to decide where to put his hands and feet.

_____ 2. Without good eyesight, many sports are impossible. Most people might think that mountain climbing is one of those sports. But Erik Weihenmayer thought differently.

_____ 3. Erik Weihenmayer, who lost his sight at age 13, later learned to climb mountains. In 2001 he was the first blind person to climb to the top of Mount Everest.

Score 4 points for each correct answer.

_____ **Total Score:** Finding the Main Idea

B. Recalling Facts

How well do you remember the facts in the article? Put an X in the box next to the answer that correctly completes each statement.

1. The first big mountain that Weihenmayer climbed was

☐ a. Mount Everest.
☐ b. Denali.
☐ c. Mount McKinley.

2. Weihenmayer made maps of mountains

☐ a. in the snow.
☐ b. on large sheets of paper.
☐ c. in his mind.

3. Weihenmayer called this "a blind person's worst nightmare":

☐ a. a field littered with chunks of ice.
☐ b. the top of Mount Everest.
☐ c. climbing up Denali.

4. Weihenmayer had little trouble climbing at night because

☐ a. he had practiced climbing at night for many years.
☐ b. since he was blind, he was used to working in the dark.
☐ c. he could see better at night than he could during the day.

Score 4 points for each correct answer.

_____ **Total Score:** Recalling Facts

C. Making Inferences

When you draw a conclusion that is not directly stated in the text, you are making an inference. Put an X in the box next to the statement that is a correct inference.

1.

☐ a. Weihenmayer was as good a climber as the other members of his team.

☐ b. None of the members of Weihenmayer's team thought he would reach the top of Everest.

☐ c. Weihenmayer never played team sports when he was a child.

2.

☐ a. Weihenmayer would have climbed just as well if he had lost both his hearing and his sight.

☐ b. Climbing Everest with Weihenmayer was much more dangerous than climbing with a sighted person.

☐ c. Weihenmayer never let his blindness stop him from doing all he could.

Score 4 points for each correct answer.

_____ **Total Score:** Making Inferences

D. Using Words

Put an X in the box next to the definition below that is closest in meaning to the underlined word.

1. My aunt is seeing a special doctor who can treat her rare disorder.

☐ a. sickness
☐ b. flowering plant
☐ c. list of books

2. After the earthquake, our house was still intact, so we let our neighbors move in with us for a few days.

☐ a. hurt or ruined
☐ b. whole or complete
☐ c. underwater

3. This burden is too heavy for me to handle alone.

☐ a. a place that is very busy
☐ b. a person who does a job well
☐ c. a load to be carried

4. During the parade, the street was littered with bits of bright paper.

☐ a. made long and narrow
☐ b. filled with things scattered around
☐ c. empty of things and people

5. The hunter's sharp eyes gave her an <u>advantage</u> in the shooting contest.

☐ a. something that makes a job harder to do well
☐ b. something that gives a better chance of success
☐ c. something that seems unfair

6. Try to <u>focus</u> on your teacher's words so you can repeat what she says.

☐ a. give attention to
☐ b. think about something else
☐ c. cover up or hide

Score 4 points for each correct answer.

_____ **Total Score:** Using Words

E. Author's Approach

Put an X in the box next to the correct answer.

1. The main purpose of the first paragraph is to

☐ a. tell who got Erik Weihenmayer interested in mountain climbing.
☐ b. show that Erik Weihenmayer was happy that he went blind.
☐ c. tell how blindness changed Erik Weihenmayer's life.

2. What is the author's purpose in writing this article?

☐ a. to get the reader to learn to climb high mountains
☐ b. to tell the reader how to climb Mount Everest
☐ c. to tell what happened when one man refused to give up

3. From the statements below, choose the one that you believe the author would agree with.

☐ a. Everyone on the 10-man team except Erik found the climb up Everest to be easy.
☐ b. Climbing Mount Everest is difficult even for the best climbers.
☐ c. Erik Weihenmayer always used his blindness as an excuse to not try things that were hard.

Score 4 points for each correct answer.

_____ **Total Score:** Author's Approach

F. Summarizing and Paraphrasing

Put an X in the box next to the correct answer.

1. Which summary says all the important things about the article?

☐ a. Erik Weihenmayer overcame problems to climb high mountains. On one climb, he crossed a big ice field filled with chunks of ice. He also waited out a big storm.

☐ b. Erik Weihenmayer, blind since 13, climbed high mountains all over the world. In 2001 he was part of a 10-man team that climbed Mount Everest. He became the first blind person to reach its summit.

☐ c. In 2001 Erik Weihenmayer climbed Mount Everest. Jeff Evans also reached the top. He lost 30 pounds on the way. Eric Alexander and Brad Bull overcame fears and worries to join them at the summit.

2. Which sentence means the same thing as the following sentence? "But everyone on the team overcame something to get there."

☐ a. Each team member had to work hard to reach the top.

☐ b. Every team member traveled a long way to reach Mount Everest.

☐ c. All the team members enjoyed climbing Everest.

Score 4 points for each correct answer.

_____ **Total Score:** Summarizing and Paraphrasing

G. Critical Thinking

Put an X in the box next to the correct answer.

1. Choose the statement below that states an opinion.

☐ a. Mountain climbing is a sport that only people in perfect shape should try.

☐ b. Weihenmayer took less time to cross the ice field on his fifth trip than he did on his first trip.

☐ c. Some of the climbers had trouble when they could not see their feet.

2. From information in the article, you can predict that

☐ a. no one will ever want to climb a mountain with Weihenmayer again.

☐ b. Weihenmayer will stop liking dangerous sports.

☐ c. Weihenmayer will keep trying new things.

3. Jeff Evans and Brad Bull are alike because they both

☐ a. had climbed Denali.

☐ b. overcame a problem.

☐ c. had lost 30 pounds.

4. On the way up Everest, the climbers found chunks of ice scattered all over a field. What was the effect of the wild way the chunks were scattered?

☐ a. Weihenmayer became the first blind person to reach the summit of Everest.

☐ b. The climbers had to put on special glasses and oxygen masks.

☐ c. Weihenmayer had a problem because he could not predict where the ice chunks would be.

5. Which lesson about life does this story teach?

☐ a. Focus on what you are able to do, not what you can't do.

☐ b. To be happy, try only those things that you are sure you can do easily and quickly.

☐ c. Accept that there are many things that you will never be able to do.

Score 4 points for each correct answer.

_____ **Total Score:** Critical Thinking

Enter your score for each activity. Add the scores together. Record your total score on the graph on page 115.

_____ Finding the Main Idea

_____ Recalling Facts

_____ Making Inferences

_____ Using Words

_____ Author's Approach

_____ Summarizing and Paraphrasing

_____ Critical Thinking

_____ **Total Score**

Personal Response

Describe a time when you overcame a problem to reach a goal. _____

_____

_____

Self-Assessment

When reading the article, I was having trouble with

_____

_____

One Dangerous Job

In a strange way, things worked out for the best for Jim Severence. A fishing trap fell on him and smashed his leg. The same trap also fractured the skull of a shipmate. Severence took the events as a warning. So he quit his job. "I figured I used up my luck and got out," he said. "I've lost a lot of friends."

2   Severence was a crab fisherman. He fished for king crab in the Bering Sea off the coast of Alaska. Experts say crab fishing is the most dangerous job in the United States. It is 16 times more deadly than police work. The number of deaths varies from year to year. But it is common for 15 or more fishermen to die each season. The 1988 season was a really bad one. In the port of Kodiak, the church bell rings for each death on a crab fishing boat. That year it rang 44 times.

3   The people who go crab fishing know the risks. They must accept them. "When we leave town for the sea," said Minh Vu, "we know some are not coming back."

4   Brian Bugg was one of those who didn't make it back home. On April 3, 1992, 25-year-old Bugg was working

Crab fishermen battle high winds and rough water on the Bering Sea.

with a crab trap. Even when empty, these traps weigh up to 750 pounds each. A full trap can weigh 2,000 pounds. It takes a crane and hook to lift a full trap out of the sea and onto a fishing boat.

5   This time something went wrong with the hook. The trap broke free and plunged back into the water. Bugg rushed to help. He tried to grab the rope that was attached to the trap, but his feet got tangled in it. As the trap fell to the bottom of the sea, the rope tightened around his feet. In an instant he was yanked over the side and down toward the ocean floor. It happened in a flash. No one could save him. Brian Bugg was the 12th fisherman to die that year.

6   Sometimes it's not a single fisherman who dies. Sometimes it's the whole crew. In 1996 a crab boat called the *Pacesetter* headed out into the Bering Sea. Its captain was Matthew Pope. Pope had spent 10 years at sea. He knew what he was doing. His boat was large— 127 feet long—and it was in perfect shape. But none of that mattered when a big storm hit. The boat capsized. When it turned over, all seven men were lost. The boat, too, vanished. A couple of empty life rafts were later recovered, along with a few pieces of equipment. But that was it. No other trace of the boat or its crew was ever found.

7   "I know that he didn't think it would happen to him," said Pope's wife, Pamela. But Pope was fooling himself. Dale Lindsey, the owner of the *Pacesetter*, said what every crab fisherman knows. "In the fishing industry, sometimes things like this happen."

8   One of the dangers on crab boats is ice. The fishing season comes in winter. The Bering Sea is very cold. Heavy ice often coats the deck of the boat. If too much ice builds up, the boat becomes top heavy. It can then tip over easily. Fishermen try to break up the ice on deck with baseball bats and iron bars. But they never get it all. The deck is always slippery. So walking across it is no easy task. To make matters worse, the boat sometimes rocks wildly. During storms it is tossed by waves as high as buildings with five levels.

9   Fatigue is yet another problem. Crab fishermen don't get much sleep. They work up to 20 hours a day. They do this day after day. Says one fisherman, "You get so tired, you kind of cry to yourself." A tired fisherman is more likely to make a mistake. And on the Bering Sea, even a small mistake can kill.

10   Crab fishermen could reduce the risks if they waited for calm seas and clear skies. But they can't wait for good weather. There is a limit to how many tons of crabs can be caught each year. When that limit is reached, all crab fishing must end. So it's a race to see which boats can bring in the most. It doesn't matter how rough the sea is. As soon as the season opens, all the boats rush out. A person who knows the job well might say it is an accident waiting to happen.

11   Still, every year people sign up to work on crab boats. Some like the thrill of it. They think of themselves as the "cowboys of the sea." Beyond that, the money is good. Crab fishermen can make a lot of money in just two months. For many people, it's the only good-paying job around. Phil Hanson, the father of a fisherman, says he knows people who wouldn't go out fishing if they had enough money to stay home. He says, "You just know someone's going to get hurt."

A. Finding the Main Idea

One statement below tells the main idea of the article. One statement is too general, or too broad. The other statement explains only part of the article; it is too narrow. Label the statements using the following key:

M—Main Idea   B—Too Broad   N—Too Narrow

_____ 1. Brian Bugg was one of the unlucky crab fishermen who didn't make it back home. His feet tangled up in a rope. He was dragged down toward the bottom of the ocean.

_____ 2. It is really sad when a person dies on the job. Some jobs are more dangerous than others.

_____ 3. Crab fishing may be the most dangerous job in the United States. Fishermen must battle problems with the boat, weather, and their tired bodies to get home safely.

Score 4 points for each correct answer.

_____ **Total Score:** Finding the Main Idea

B. Recalling Facts

How well do you remember the facts in the article? Put an X in the box next to the answer that correctly completes each statement.

1. In 1988, the church bell in the port of Kodiak rang
   ☐ a. 15 times.
   ☐ b. 26 times.
   ☐ c. 44 times.

2. When a crab boat called the *Pacesetter* turned over,
   ☐ a. seven men died.
   ☐ b. 15 men died.
   ☐ c. 12 men died.

3. Crab fishermen work quickly so that they can
   ☐ a. get home before the cold weather sets in.
   ☐ b. catch as many crabs as possible.
   ☐ c. keep their boats from capsizing.

4. Crab fishermen can make a lot of money in just
   ☐ a. six months.
   ☐ b. two weeks.
   ☐ c. two months.

Score 4 points for each correct answer.

_____ **Total Score:** Recalling Facts

C. Making Inferences

When you draw a conclusion that is not directly stated in the text, you are making an inference. Put an X in the box next to the statement that is a correct inference.

1.

☐ a. All crab fishermen really enjoy their jobs and wouldn't want to do anything else.

☐ b. People who want to be sure they are safe on the job should stay away from crab fishing.

☐ c. There is no good reason why crab fishing can't be done in the summer, when the weather is fine.

2.

☐ a. Crab fishing is the only way to earn money in Kodiak, Alaska.

☐ b. On a crab boat, there is plenty of free time for the fishermen to rest and relax.

☐ c. For some crab fishermen, the danger of the job makes the work exciting.

Score 4 points for each correct answer.

_____ **Total Score:** Making Inferences

D. Using Words

Put an X in the box next to the definition below that is closest in meaning to the underlined word.

1. The skater's arm was <u>fractured</u> in two places when she fell on the ice.

☐ a. made whole
☐ b. cracked
☐ c. killed

2. Everything fell into the water when the boat <u>capsized</u>.

☐ a. turned over
☐ b. tied up at the dock
☐ c. set out on a trip

3. Divers were glad when they <u>recovered</u> gold pieces from the ship that sank.

☐ a. ruined
☐ b. found again
☐ c. lost again

4. The steel <u>industry</u> gives many people jobs in our city.

☐ a. reward
☐ b. story
☐ c. business

5. Police said that the driver's <u>fatigue</u> made him fall asleep at the wheel.

☐ a. state of being tired
☐ b. state of being angry
☐ c. state of being too busy

6. The doctor says you can <u>reduce</u> the swelling if you put your foot up.

☐ a. make more
☐ b. make less
☐ c. make worse

> Score 4 points for each correct answer.
>
> _____ **Total Score:** Using Words

E. | Author's Approach

Put an X in the box next to the correct answer.

1. What is the author's purpose in writing this article?

☐ a. to get the reader to become a crab fisherman
☐ b. to tell what a dangerous job crab fishing is
☐ c. to describe what happens when ice builds up on a boat

2. Choose the statement below that is the weakest argument for becoming a crab fisherman.

☐ a. Crab fishermen can earn a lot of money in a short time.
☐ b. Many crab fishermen die on the job.
☐ c. Crab fishing can be exciting.

3. Choose the statement below that best describes the author's opinion in paragraph 11.

☐ a. Even though crab fishing is dangerous, some people want to or need to do it.
☐ b. Crab fishermen sometimes cause their own problems by acting like "cowboys of the sea."
☐ c. Most crab fishermen make so much money in only two months that they never have to work again.

> Score 4 points for each correct answer.
>
> _____ **Total Score:** Author's Approach

F. Summarizing and Paraphrasing

Put an X in the box next to the correct answer.

1. Which summary says all the important things about the article?

☐ a. Crab fishermen battle ice, bad weather, fatigue, and bad luck to do their jobs on the Bering Sea off the coast of Alaska. Many of them die during the short fishing season.

☐ b. People fish for crabs in the Bering Sea off the coast of Alaska. They get paid well for their jobs. If the job didn't pay so well, many people would quit.

☐ c. One of the things that makes crab fishing so dangerous is the weather. In the winter, ice builds up on the crab boats. Fishermen must break up the ice with baseball bats or iron bars.

2. Which sentence means the same thing as the following sentence? "There is a limit to how many tons of crabs can be caught each year."

☐ a. There is a limited number of crabs in the ocean each year.

☐ b. Fishermen set limits as to how many crabs they want to catch each year.

☐ c. Fishermen are allowed to catch only a limited amount of crabs every year.

G. Critical Thinking

Put an X in the box next to the correct answer.

1. Choose the statement below that states an opinion.

☐ a. An empty crab trap can weigh up to 750 pounds, and a full trap can weigh 2,000 pounds.

☐ b. Crab fishermen have the hardest job of all the workers in the world.

☐ c. Crab fishermen often work as many as 20 hours in one day.

2. Jim Severence and Brian Bugg are different because

☐ a. only Bugg was a crab fisherman.

☐ b. only Severence was hurt on the job.

☐ c. only Bugg was pulled underwater.

3. What is an effect of the building up of ice on a crab boat?

☐ a. The boat may get top heavy and tip over.

☐ b. The fishermen must pull up the traps quickly.

☐ c. The fishermen can trap more crabs.

4. Which paragraph provides information that supports your answer to question 3?

☐ a. paragraph 2

☐ b. paragraph 8

☐ c. paragraph 10

Score 4 points for each correct answer.

_____ **Total Score:** Summarizing and Paraphrasing

5. How is crab fishing an example of going into the danger zone?

- ☐ a. Crab fishermen go to work knowing that they may be killed on the job.
- ☐ b. Crab fishermen can earn quite a bit of money, especially since they work only two months.
- ☐ c. To catch crabs, fishermen use heavy traps that can weigh as much as 750 pounds.

Score 4 points for each correct answer.

_____ **Total Score:** Critical Thinking

Enter your score for each activity. Add the scores together. Record your total score on the graph on page 115.

_____ Finding the Main Idea

_____ Recalling Facts

_____ Making Inferences

_____ Using Words

_____ Author's Approach

_____ Summarizing and Paraphrasing

_____ Critical Thinking

_____ **Total Score**

Personal Response

What was most surprising or interesting to you about this article? _____

_____

_____

Self-Assessment

While reading the article, _____

_____

_____ was the easiest for me.

Compare and Contrast

Pick two stories in Unit Two that tell about people who showed great courage in the face of danger. Use information from the stories to fill in this chart.

Title	Did the person choose to go into danger, or was there no choice?	How did the person show his or her courage?	Do you think this person will go into danger again? Explain your thinking.

Which person do you admire most? Write a letter to him or her. Tell why you admire him or her. _____

_____

_____

UNIT THREE

Not Part of the Act

Shown here is Oscar Garcia performing on the revolving wheel just minutes before falling 25 feet to the ground.

Higigh-flying circus acts are risky. That's why people love them so much. Audiences love to see acrobats jump and spin. They love to watch performers do their stunts high in the air. Circus acrobats start with fairly simple stunts. Then they work up to more dangerous ones. The last stunt of each act is often the most dangerous.

2   Most of the time, everything goes smoothly. People cheer and clap and walk away wondering how the acrobats do it. But once in a while an act doesn't go as planned. That happened to Oscar Garcia. His act was called the "Wheel of Destiny." As this name suggests, Garcia found that his success depended on luck. He jumped rope and walked blindfolded on a moving wheel. The wheel spun high off the ground in what Garcia called "a thrill act."

3   Garcia had performed this stunt hundreds of times, but he never forgot the dangers. That's why he always said a prayer first. "Friends say I look happy up there," he said. "But every time I go up, I'm scared."

4   On June 10, 1989, Garcia was in St. Louis. He was performing in a circus held at Busch Stadium, the famous sports arena. As usual, he said a prayer and then got up on the wheel. Everything seemed to be going well. But near the end, Garcia made a mistake. "I got carried away," he said, "and was running too fast."

5   Garcia lost his balance. He struggled to stay on top of the wheel, and then he tried to grab the side of it, but it was no use. Garcia fell 20 feet to the ground. "When I hit the floor, the air came out of my body. My arms started to swell," he recalled.

6   His wife, Kathy, who witnessed the accident, said, "That Busch Stadium floor has padding. That's why he's not more seriously hurt." Still, Kathy said her husband "bounced a clear foot" off the floor. Garcia was lucky he didn't die. However, he did break several bones, and he shattered his elbow. "Maybe if it happens again, I won't be so lucky," he said.

7   After 15 years in the circus, Oscar Garcia accepts the dangers that are part of his job. Even after his near deadly fall, he has made no plans to change careers. "I'll definitely stay in the circus," he said. "It's my life."

8   His wife agrees. "If it's in your heart, you go back and do it again," she said.

9   The circus was in acrobat Kristie Randall's heart too. Randall was known as "The Phantom of the Air." She almost looked like a ghost as she hung far above the ground. Her act included a spin called the "hanging perch." For this stunt, she dangled from a rope high in the air. The 19-year-old's head was held in place by a ring around her neck as the rope spun her wildly. To add a little extra excitement, Randall did not use a net to catch her if she fell.

10 Randall's act was very successful. But on April 10, 1994, something went wrong. She was in a circus in St. Paul, Minnesota. Somehow the ring slipped off her neck. Randall fell 60 feet. She hit the concrete floor with a loud thud. "It's a sound that I'll never forget," said ringmaster Peter Sturgis, a circus announcer.

11 The audience couldn't believe it. One man said, "I could hear people around me saying, 'Oh, it's just part of the act.' That was my feeling right away."

12 But people soon understood it was not part of the act. They were amazed that Randall had lived through such an accident. A fall from that high should have killed her, but it didn't. Kristie Randall got away with just a broken hip, back, and elbow. "It's a miracle that I'm alive," she said.

13 People expect strange things to happen at the circus. They see stunts that seem incredible. So when something does go wrong, they don't always know it. As with Kristie Randall's accident, they often think it's "part of the act."

14 Take the case of Jacques Mbembo, an acrobat from Gabon in Africa. On April 13, 1998, he was performing in a leopard skin and grass skirt. At one point he was jumping over a burning rope. It was a funny act. The audience loved it.

15 Then, suddenly, Mbembo's skirt caught fire. He dropped to the ground and began to roll around. He was trying to snuff out the flames. Most people didn't understand that he was in trouble. Finally Mbembo ran out of the circus ring. "He was still on fire when he ran out," said one man. "At first I thought it was part of the act."

16 At last people realized the truth. "It was awful," said one woman. "He was in flames and screaming. Then we started to scream."

17 "I thought it was very scary when I smelled the smoke," said an eight-year-old boy. "He was all on fire."

18 Luckily, one of the ringmasters was able to put out the flames. But by then Mbembo had suffered some bad burns.

19 Everyone who works in the circus knows that such accidents can happen at any time. As circus owner George Hamid said, "The nature of the business is danger. . . . Aerial acts are dangerous. That's show business."

A. Finding the Main Idea

One statement below tells the main idea of the article. One statement is too general, or too broad. The other statement explains only part of the article; it is too narrow. Label the statements using the following key:

M—Main Idea   B—Too Broad   N—Too Narrow

_____ 1. When mistakes happen at the circus, it is not just part of the act. Accidents at the circus can hurt or even kill performers.

_____ 2. Some people's jobs are dangerous. Just going to work leads to risks that most people would not want to take.

_____ 3. Kristie Randall had an act the audience loved. She put her head into a ring and spun wildly, high above the ground. Because she did not use a net, the act was truly dangerous.

Score 4 points for each correct answer.

_____ **Total Score:** Finding the Main Idea

B. Recalling Facts

How well do you remember the facts in the article? Put an X in the box next to the answer that correctly completes each statement.

1. Oscar Garcia fell off the moving wheel after
   - ☐ a. the wheel suddenly stopped spinning.
   - ☐ b. the wheel started wobbling wildly.
   - ☐ c. he ran too fast and lost his balance.

2. Kristie Randall was known as
   - ☐ a. "The Phantom of the Air."
   - ☐ b. "The Princess of the High Wire."
   - ☐ c. "The Queen of Destiny."

3. In her accident, Kristie Randall suffered
   - ☐ a. a shattered leg and ankle.
   - ☐ b. a broken hip, back, and elbow.
   - ☐ c. memory loss when her head hit the floor.

4. Jacques Mbembo's grass skirt caught fire when
   - ☐ a. he jumped over a burning rope.
   - ☐ b. he dropped a burning stick on the skirt.
   - ☐ c. the ringmaster accidentally dropped a match on Mbembo's skirt.

Score 4 points for each correct answer.

_____ **Total Score:** Recalling Facts

C. Making Inferences

When you draw a conclusion that is not directly stated in the text, you are making an inference. Put an X in the box next to the statement that is a correct inference.

1.

☐ a. Kathy Garcia could not watch her husband's act because it made her too nervous.

☐ b. Oscar Garcia worked without a net below him.

☐ c. If Oscar Garcia could find any other job, he would certainly take it.

2.

☐ a. Once audience members knew that Mbembo was really in trouble, they ran to help him.

☐ b. Now that circus owner George Hamid realizes that his circus is dangerous, he will probably close it.

☐ c. It's hard for audience members to know what is a part of the act and what is an accident at the circus.

Score 4 points for each correct answer.

_____ **Total Score:** Making Inferences

D. Using Words

Put an X in the box next to the definition below that is closest in meaning to the underlined word.

1. Acrobats must stay in good shape so they can do their tricks safely.

☐ a. people who perform tricks on the ground or high in the air

☐ b. people who watch TV news or listen to radio news every day

☐ c. people who are afraid of heights

2. Some people do crazy stunts, such as swimming in ice-cold water, just to get on the TV news.

☐ a. jokes, riddles, or other funny stories

☐ b. tricks that show skill or daring

☐ c. household chores that must be done every day

3. I was standing on the corner, and I witnessed the accident that happened there.

☐ a. traveled

☐ b. loosened

☐ c. saw

4. The girl shattered the mirror when she dropped it on the floor.

☐ a. broke into many pieces

☐ b. hung on the wall

☐ c. decorated with flowers

5. It seems <u>incredible</u> to have snow in the summer, but snow really did fall on the Fourth of July.

☐ a. easy to believe and accept
☐ b. not possible to believe
☐ c. old-fashioned or out of date

6. The mayor went up in a small plane to get an <u>aerial</u> view of the storm damage.

☐ a. having to do with flying
☐ b. having to do with rivers or lakes
☐ c. having to do with weather

Score 4 points for each correct answer.

_____ **Total Score:** Using Words

E. Author's Approach

Put an X in the box next to the correct answer.

1. The main purpose of the first paragraph is to

☐ a. explain why acrobats love their jobs so much.
☐ b. tell about an accident that happened to Oscar Garcia.
☐ c. describe the acts that high-flying acrobats do.

2. The author probably wrote this article in order to

☐ a. let readers know that not everything goes as planned in the circus.
☐ b. get readers to become circus acrobats.
☐ c. get readers upset about the dangers of circus life, so they will stop going to circuses.

3. The author tells this story mainly by

☐ a. describing the experiences of different performers.
☐ b. telling about what happened to one person, in time order.
☐ c. using his or her imagination.

Score 4 points for each correct answer.

_____ **Total Score:** Author's Approach

F. | Summarizing and Paraphrasing

Put an X in the box next to the correct answer.

1. Which summary says all the important things about the article?

☐ a. Oscar Garcia knows the risks that come with his job. In fact, he always says a prayer before he begins his act. People say he was lucky he didn't die in a bad fall from a wheel that spun high above the ground.

☐ b. Oscar Garcia, Kristie Randall, and Jacques Mbembo all put themselves in danger. Even though they were careful, accidents almost took their lives.

☐ c. Circus acrobats can risk their lives in every act. Acrobat Oscar Garcia fell from a high wheel and broke bones. Kristie Randall barely lived through a bad fall. Jacques Mbembo suffered burns in his act.

2. Which sentence means the same thing as the following sentence? "For this stunt, she dangled from a rope high in the air."

☐ a. To do this stunt, she dangled a rope high above the circus floor.

☐ b. When she did this stunt, she hung from a rope high above the circus floor.

☐ c. The rope dangled high above her as she did this stunt.

Score 4 points for each correct answer.

_____ **Total Score:** Summarizing and Paraphrasing

G. | Critical Thinking

Put an X in the box next to the correct answer.

1. Choose the statement below that states a fact.

☐ a. Acrobats are the bravest performers in the circus.

☐ b. In 1989 Oscar Garcia fell 20 feet and broke several bones.

☐ c. People should not risk their lives just to entertain other people.

2. From information in the article, you can predict that

☐ a. soon no one will watch circus acts because they are too dangerous.

☐ b. soon no one will want to be a circus performer because the job is too risky.

☐ c. there will always be someone who likes doing dangerous acts to entertain others.

3. Oscar Garcia and Kristie Randall are alike because

☐ a. both had bad accidents in Busch Stadium in St. Louis.

☐ b. both died in a fall to the circus floor.

☐ c. both fell to the circus floor and were badly hurt.

4. Jacques Mbembo rolled around on the ground during his act in 1998. What was the cause of his action?

☐ a. He was trying to put out the fire on his skirt.

☐ b. He was trying to make the audience laugh.

☐ c. He was pretending that the fire on his skirt was a real problem.

5. Which paragraph provides information that supports your answer to question 4?

☐ a. paragraph 14

☐ b. paragraph 15

☐ c. paragraph 18

Score 4 points for each correct answer.

_____ **Total Score:** Critical Thinking

Enter your score for each activity. Add the scores together. Record your total score on the graph on page 115.

_____ Finding the Main Idea

_____ Recalling Facts

_____ Making Inferences

_____ Using Words

_____ Author's Approach

_____ Summarizing and Paraphrasing

_____ Critical Thinking

_____ **Total Score**

Personal Response

I wonder why _____

_____

_____

Self-Assessment

Before reading this article, I already knew _____

_____

_____

Skeleton Racing

"I couldn't miss the Games," said Alex Coomber. "I had to compete, and I had to win a medal." Coomber knew that everyone in Great Britain was counting on her. After all, she was placed at number one in the world. "The whole of Britain would have said that I was a failure if I'd come back with nothing."

2   Coomber was competing in the 2002 Winter Olympic Games in Park City, Utah. The British don't win many medals in winter sports. That's why they were excited to have Coomber on their team. They knew she had the skill and drive to win a gold medal.

3   There was just one problem. Coomber had broken her arm in a training run two weeks before the Games opened. She could tell the arm was broken because the pain was tremendous, but she didn't say a word. She knew that if her trainers found out, they would not let her compete. So she kept quiet and tried to ignore the pain.

4   Coomber's event was skeleton racing. Skeleton racers lie on a sled and shoot down an icy course filled with

sharp turns and steep drops. Top racers can reach speeds of over 80 miles an hour. At such speeds, skeleton racing is dangerous. In fact, it was once considered so dangerous it was banned. The last Olympic skeleton race had been in 1948. For many years the sport was not allowed in the Olympics, but now it was back.

5   Speed isn't the only danger. The sled itself adds to the risk. First of all, it has no brakes. The sled stops only when the course ends or when the racer crashes. And there are plenty of crashes. "I know a lot of people watch the sport to wait for the crashes," said Coomber. "I don't mind that."

6   Then there is the problem of steering. A skeleton sled doesn't have any steering mechanism, so racers must try to direct it by leaning to one side or the other. Coomber said she is in control about "95 percent" of the time. What happens during the other five percent? "You have very, very small parts of seconds when you feel out of control," she admitted.

7   The racers lie on their stomachs. They go down the course headfirst. Their chins are just an inch or two off the ice. "Imagine a roller coaster going twice the speed it normally does," said one racer known as Dr. Ice. "You're hanging off the front with no seat belt. . . . It's as scary as that every time you go down."

Shown here is an athlete training for the skeleton event in the 2002 Winter Olympics.

8 At the start of the course, racers pick up the sled in their hands. Then they run up to the starting line and plop themselves down on the sled. Tristan Gale said it's like "tying yourself to an airplane wing." But then Gale suggested that everyone should try it at least once in his or her lifetime. "There's nothing like this, like skeleton, in real life," she said. "After you finish, your eyeballs are huge!"

9 Coomber first tried skeleton racing when she was 22 years old. It took her just one run to fall in love with it. And she was good at it. Within a week, she was competing and winning.

10 Now she was off to the Olympics. Coomber's arm still hurt a lot. But her biggest concern was the weather. On February 20, the day of the big race, it was snowing. Snow on the course, Coomber said, "acts like sandpaper." It "slows you down." Snow was especially tough for Coomber. That's because she weighed less than most other racers. She had more trouble controlling her sled on a snowy course. Heavier women could battle through the snow and go down the course more easily. Said Coomber, "If you're small, like me, the snow is an absolute disaster."

11 Andreas Schmind, Coomber's coach, said, "We knew that the bad weather would be a factor against her. But Alex is such a fearless rider. We still had confidence in her."

12 Also, there were 15,000 fans cheering her on. Among them were her two little nephews. They held up a banner that read, "Go, Aunty Alex, Go."

13 So despite the broken arm and the snow, Coomber decided to give it her best try. "I convinced myself I could go well in the snow," she said.

14 Each racer goes down the course twice. The winner is the one with the fastest combined time. On her first run, Coomber hit the walls on the turns several times. But as she later said, she "just kept holding on, hoping for a quick time." She finished in a very fast time. After her second run, Coomber was in first place. There were only two racers to go. But both had terrific runs and beat Coomber.

15 Coomber didn't win the gold medal, but her third place finish was enough to earn her the bronze medal. That made her happy. "It is a fantastic feeling to get the bronze," she said.

16 Her mother, Rosemary, was delighted too. "I cried when I knew she had got a medal of some sort," she said. "I am just so proud."

17 After the race, Coomber finally had a doctor examine her arm. The break was a bad one. By continuing to use her arm, Coomber had made it worse. It would now take a long time to heal. But for Alex Coomber, this was a small price to pay. She was going back to Great Britain with an Olympic medal.

A. Finding the Main Idea

One statement below tells the main idea of the article. One statement is too general, or too broad. The other statement explains only part of the article; it is too narrow. Label the statements using the following key:

M—Main Idea   B—Too Broad   N—Too Narrow

_____ 1. An Olympic athlete from Great Britain ignored the pain from a broken arm to compete in the 2002 Winter Olympic Games. In her event, skeleton racing, she won a bronze medal.

_____ 2. In order to win and bring honor to their countries, many Olympic athletes do their best in spite of pain.

_____ 3. Alex Coomber competed in the skeleton racing event in the 2002 Winter Olympic Games in Park City, Utah. She knew that skeleton racing was dangerous. It had been banned from the Olympics for years before returning in 2002.

Score 4 points for each correct answer.

_____ **Total Score:** Finding the Main Idea

B. Recalling Facts

How well do you remember the facts in the article? Put an X in the box next to the answer that correctly completes each statement.

1. Alex Coomber had broken her arm

☐ a. in a skiing accident.
☐ b. during training.
☐ c. in a race car crash.

2. The British really wanted to win a medal because

☐ a. they had always won a medal in skeleton racing.
☐ b. they knew Coomber had broken her arm and thought that winning the medal would make her feel better.
☐ c. they hardly ever win any medals in winter sports.

3. You control a skeleton sled by

☐ a. leaning from side to side.
☐ b. pushing a control bar.
☐ c. turning a steering wheel.

4. On the day of the race there was a snowfall, so

☐ a. Coomber knew that her chances of winning were better than ever.
☐ b. Coomber had trouble controlling her sled.
☐ c. heavier racers had a harder time staying on track than Coomber did.

Score 4 points for each correct answer.

_____ **Total Score:** Recalling Facts

C. Making Inferences

When you draw a conclusion that is not directly stated in the text, you are making an inference. Put an X in the box next to the statement that is a correct inference.

1.

☐ a. For Alex Coomber, winning a medal was more important than her health.

☐ b. People who are afraid when they compete in a sport can never win.

☐ c. All it takes to win an Olympic medal is enthusiasm and courage.

2.

☐ a. Alex Coomber never settles for anything but the top prize in whatever she does.

☐ b. When it snows, Olympic officials stop the skeleton race because it becomes too dangerous.

☐ c. Coomber's British friends were probably proud of her, even though she didn't win the gold medal.

Score 4 points for each correct answer.

_____ **Total Score:** Making Inferences

D. Using Words

Put an X in the box next to the definition below that is closest in meaning to the underlined word.

1. My aunt is happiest when she is busy and active. She certainly has the drive needed to get the job done.

☐ a. lack of interest
☐ b. anger
☐ c. energy

2. We can't get the car going because the mechanism that starts the motor is broken.

☐ a. directions that explain how something works
☐ b. parts of a machine that work together
☐ c. a type of oil needed by engines

3. People who saw that movie complained that it was an absolute waste of time.

☐ a. complete
☐ b. pleasant
☐ c. friendly

4. All the passengers had confidence that the pilot would get them home safely.

☐ a. strong feeling of sorrow or fear
☐ b. strong dislike of a person or thing
☐ c. strong trust in a person or thing

5. My father won because his score by itself was more than the scores of my brother and me <u>combined</u>.

☐ a. one by one
☐ b. put together
☐ c. correctly

6. The twins had a <u>fantastic</u> time at their birthday party and were happy the whole week after it.

☐ a. hard to believe but wonderful
☐ b. terrible but expected
☐ c. likely to make someone angry

> Score 4 points for each correct answer.
>
> _____ **Total Score:** Using Words

E. Author's Approach

Put an X in the box next to the correct answer.

1. The main purpose of the first paragraph is to

☐ a. describe the sport of skeleton racing.
☐ b. explain why winning a medal was so important to Coomber.
☐ c. show how brave Alex Coomber was since she was competing with a broken arm.

2. What is the author's purpose in writing this article?

☐ a. to tell the reader about a brave athlete
☐ b. to get the reader to learn how to skeleton race
☐ c. to make the reader feel sad that Coomber didn't win the gold medal

3. From the statements below, choose the one that you believe the author would agree with.

☐ a. Alex Coomber did not care much about what people in Great Britain thought of her.
☐ b. Skeleton racing is probably pretty easy, even with a broken arm.
☐ c. People who need to be in control at all times should probably not take up skeleton racing.

> Score 4 points for each correct answer.
>
> _____ **Total Score:** Author's Approach

F. Summarizing and Paraphrasing

Put an X in the box next to the correct answer.

1. Which summary says all the important things about the article?

☐ a. Alex Coomber was the number-one skeleton racer in the world in 2002. In one important race, she came in third even though she wasn't feeling well.

☐ b. In spite of having a broken arm, British skeleton racer Alex Coomber competed in the 2002 Winter Olympic Games and won a bronze medal.

☐ c. Alex Coomber of Great Britain knew that people in her country were counting on her to bring home an Olympic medal. She did her best and won a bronze medal.

2. Which sentence means the same thing as the following sentence? "After you finish, your eyeballs are huge!"

☐ a. You are excited both during and after the race.

☐ b. You can see better after you finish the race.

☐ c. This race hurts your eyes so much that after the race you feel like you can't close them.

Score 4 points for each correct answer.

_____ **Total Score:** Summarizing and Paraphrasing

G. Critical Thinking

Put an X in the box next to the correct answer.

1. Choose the statement below that states an opinion.

☐ a. In skeleton racing, each racer goes down the course two times.

☐ b. Skeleton racers can reach speeds of over 80 miles per hour.

☐ c. Alex Coomber should have told doctors about her broken arm before the race.

2. From information in the article, you can predict that

☐ a. because Coomber got hurt training for skeleton racing, it will be banned from the Olympics again.

☐ b. Coomber will continue to believe winning is important.

☐ c. Olympic officials will take away Coomber's medal because she didn't tell the trainers she was hurt.

3. A skeleton sled and a roller coaster are alike because

☐ a. both go fast downhill.

☐ b. in both, you ride headfirst with your chin about two inches off the ground.

☐ c. riders control both with the weight of their bodies.

4. What was the effect of Coomber's decision to continue using her broken arm?

☐ a. Coomber had to go down the race course twice.

☐ b. The trainers would not let her compete in the race.

☐ c. Coomber made the break worse and harder to heal.

5. Which paragraph provides information that supports your answer to question 4?

☐ a. paragraph 3
☐ b. paragraph 17
☐ c. paragraph 10

Score 4 points for each correct answer.

_____ **Total Score:** Critical Thinking

Enter your score for each activity. Add the scores together. Record your total score on the graph on page 115.

_____ Finding the Main Idea

_____ Recalling Facts

_____ Making Inferences

_____ Using Words

_____ Author's Approach

_____ Summarizing and Paraphrasing

_____ Critical Thinking

_____ **Total Score**

Personal Response

I know how Alex Coomber felt when she thought she

might not be able to compete, because _____

_____

_____

Self-Assessment

One of the things I did best when reading this article was

_____

_____

I believe I did this well because _____

_____

_____

A Hero by Any Standard

Shown here is Matthew Lukwiya, the heroic doctor who treated victims of the dreaded Ebola virus in Gulu, Uganda.

The call came on Saturday morning. It was from St. Mary's Hospital in Gulu, Uganda. Dr. Matthew Lukwiya picked up the phone. He listened carefully.

2 "There seems to be a strange disease killing our student nurses," said a doctor on the other end of the line. The doctor asked Lukwiya to come quickly.

3 Lukwiya, or "Dr. Matthew" as he was called, was head of St. Mary's Hospital. On October 7, 2000, he was in the city of Kampala. He was taking some classes there. But when he got this message, he did not hesitate. Leaving his wife and five children in Kampala, he rushed back to Gulu. He didn't know what was wrong at St. Mary's. But he planned to find out.

4 When Dr. Matthew arrived, he learned how grim the situation was. In the past few weeks, 17 people had died hideous deaths. First they had come down with high fevers. Then they began vomiting and coughing up blood. They developed nosebleeds. They even were bleeding from their eyes and ears. Nothing seemed to help them and, after a few days, each one died. Two of the victims had been student nurses, and now a third nurse was dying the same way.

5 Dr. Matthew had never seen anything like this before. He began sifting through papers put out by the World Health Organization and the Center for Disease Control. He stayed up all night to read them. As he read, a chill must have gone down his spine. He now knew what he was facing. The deaths were caused by the dreaded Ebola virus.

6 No one knows exactly where Ebola came from. It first appeared in the 1970s in certain parts of Africa. Like any other virus, it can grow in number and cause disease once it enters a living cell. The Ebola virus passes easily from person to person. A drop of blood, a bit of sweat, a teardrop, or even a cough can pass Ebola from one victim to the next. Because of this, no one who works with Ebola victims is safe. Dr. Matthew knew that. But he would not let people down when they needed him most.

7 Dr. Matthew and his head nurse, Sister Maria Di Santo, went to work. They moved Ebola victims away from other patients. They ordered anyone caring for Ebola victims to wear protective clothing. Protective clothes, they hoped, would lessen the chances that the staff would catch the virus. Such clothing included gloves, gowns, masks, caps, and goggles. The goggles made it hard for the staff to do their job. The lenses regularly fogged up. So there were times when doctors and nurses had to take the goggles off. It was the only way they could see to read charts and to take blood samples.

8   As more and more victims arrived at the hospital, fear grew. Panic threatened to crush the staff's courage. But Dr. Matthew rallied them. "He told us to stay strong, to struggle, to fight as a team," said Dr. Yoti Zabulon. "People were scared, but he had always been a good leader, and so people lined up to fight with him."

9   For weeks, Dr. Matthew and his staff did their best to care for the victims. And they tried hard to keep the disease from spreading. Each day Dr. Matthew was at the hospital by 7:00 A.M. He didn't go home until 8:00 P.M. It was exhausting work. When his wife and children called to wish him a happy birthday in early November, he barely had the energy to talk to them.

10   By late November it seemed that the worst was over. The number of new cases began to drop. But sadly, 12 nurses were among the dead. And more were still fighting for their lives. At 5 A.M. on November 20, a nurse dying from Ebola went crazy. He jumped out of bed and started to run around. As he moved, he began coughing up blood. The staff could not quiet him, so they called Dr. Matthew. Dr. Matthew threw on his protective clothes, but he did not put on his goggles. Perhaps he was too sleepy, or perhaps he was in too much of a hurry. It may even be that he didn't think he could see well enough with them on. In any case, he was not wearing goggles as he helped get the nurse back to bed. An hour later the nurse was dead. And a few days after that, Dr. Matthew began showing signs of illness.

11   At first he hoped it was the flu. Then he hoped it was malaria, another disease that brings fever. At last he had to admit the truth. He had Ebola. The next six days were awful. The staff could not believe that their beloved leader was dying. Dr. Matthew's wife could not believe it either. But it was true. Early on the morning of December 5, Dr. Matthew became the 156th Ugandan to die of Ebola.

12   Over the next few weeks, 17 more died. But 250 victims got better. The death rate in this Ebola outbreak was much lower than in others. Best of all, by early 2001 the outbreak was over. Ebola might have killed thousands. It might have destroyed the whole city of Gulu. Thanks to Dr. Matthew, that had not happened. He had moved quickly and bravely to control the disease. It had cost him his life, but that was a price he had been willing to pay.

13   As one fellow doctor put it, "Matthew Lukwiya was a hero by any standard we care to use."

A. Finding the Main Idea

One statement below tells the main idea of the article. One statement is too general, or too broad. The other statement explains only part of the article; it is too narrow. Label the statements using the following key:

M—Main Idea   B—Too Broad   N—Too Narrow

_____ 1. When a disease such as the one caused by the Ebola virus strikes, victims must depend on good doctors and nurses to see them through.

_____ 2. In 2000, after weeks of caring for victims of the Ebola virus in Gulu, Uganda, Dr. Matthew Lukwiya died of the disease.

_____ 3. Everyone who worked with Ebola patients was supposed to wear clothes that would protect them. Matthew Lukwiya wore the clothes most of the time. But once he did not wear goggles.

Score 4 points for each correct answer.

_____ **Total Score:** Finding the Main Idea

B. Recalling Facts

How well do you remember the facts in the article? Put an X in the box next to the answer that correctly completes each statement.

1. The Ebola virus first appeared in the

☐ a. 1970s.
☐ b. 1980s.
☐ c. 1990s.

2. Wearing goggles made it hard for the staff to do their jobs because the goggles

☐ a. were too tight.
☐ b. were itchy.
☐ c. fogged up.

3. Everyone was afraid of the Ebola virus because

☐ a. victims could live with it for many years, but it always killed them.
☐ b. it spread easily and usually killed its victims quickly.
☐ c. the disease gave its victims a rash and made them look ugly for many years.

4. Dr. Matthew died very soon after he

☐ a. left his goggles off when helping a dying nurse.
☐ b. caught a disease called malaria.
☐ c. studied papers from the World Health Organization.

Score 4 points for each correct answer.

_____ **Total Score:** Recalling Facts

C. Making Inferences

When you draw a conclusion that is not directly stated in the text, you are making an inference. Put an X in the box next to the statement that is a correct inference.

1.

☐ a. Dr. Matthew made many wise decisions about how to care for Ebola victims.

☐ b. By doing his work, Dr. Matthew put his wife and children at greater risk of catching the Ebola virus.

☐ c. Most likely, anyone who comes down with a fever and starts vomiting is a victim of the Ebola virus.

2.

☐ a. The doctors probably knew exactly how each victim had caught the Ebola virus.

☐ b. It was easy to find people who were eager to work with the victims of the Ebola virus.

☐ c. Dr. Matthew was usually the person that the staff at St. Mary's called upon to handle big problems.

Score 4 points for each correct answer.

_____ **Total Score:** Making Inferences

D. Using Words

Put an X in the box next to the definition below that is closest in meaning to the underlined word.

1. In a contest, good spellers sometimes <u>hesitate</u> for a moment to think before they finally spell a word.

☐ a. act as quickly as possible

☐ b. look a word up in a dictionary

☐ c. hold back before acting

2. The <u>hideous</u> monster frightened everyone who saw it.

☐ a. wonderful or pretty

☐ b. horrible or ugly

☐ c. common or normal

3. Luckily, the <u>dreaded</u> visit to the dentist turned out to be not as painful as the boy had expected.

☐ a. causing fear or worry

☐ b. causing a pleasant feeling

☐ c. looked forward to eagerly

4. People who use power saws should wear <u>goggles</u>, because the dust that is raised can get into their eyes.

☐ a. heavy gloves that protect the hands of a worker

☐ b. special shoes that fit tightly around a worker's feet

☐ c. large eyeglasses that fit tightly around eyes to protect them

5. An <u>outbreak</u> of bad colds has kept many students sick in bed for the last few days.

- ☐ a. a goal that a large group of people work toward
- ☐ b. a change that is welcomed by everyone
- ☐ c. a sudden happening, usually of something unwanted

6. When their <u>beloved</u> leader died, many people cried for days.

- ☐ a. hardly known
- ☐ b. greatly loved
- ☐ c. deeply hated

Score 4 points for each correct answer.

_____ **Total Score:** Using Words

E. Author's Approach

Put an X in the box next to the correct answer.

1. The author uses the first sentence of the article to

- ☐ a. make readers wonder why the Saturday call was important.
- ☐ b. describe Dr. Matthew Lukwiya as a fine doctor.
- ☐ c. compare Dr. Matthew Lukwiya and another doctor at St. Mary's Hospital.

2. What is the author's purpose in writing this article?

- ☐ a. to get the reader to give money to the World Health Organization
- ☐ b. to tell the reader about a brave and caring doctor
- ☐ c. to describe what happens when a person gets sick in Africa

3. Choose the statement below that best describes the author's opinion in paragraph 12.

- ☐ a. This Ebola outbreak was the worst tragedy in the history of mankind.
- ☐ b. Because of Dr. Matthew, many people's lives were saved.
- ☐ c. It is impossible for anyone to control the spread of the Ebola virus.

Score 4 points for each correct answer.

_____ **Total Score:** Author's Approach

F. Summarizing and Paraphrasing

Put an X in the box next to the correct answer.

1. Which summary says all the important things about the article?

☐ a. In late 2000, the Ebola virus was killing people in Gulu, Uganda. Dr. Matthew Lukwiya spent weeks caring for the victims and making sure the disease didn't spread. He himself died of the disease.

☐ b. The Ebola virus can spread easily. It can pass from person to person in blood, sweat, a teardrop, or a cough. That is why the disease is hard to control.

☐ c. To stop the spread of the Ebola virus in 2000, Dr. Matthew Lukwiya ordered people to wear protective clothing. They wore gowns, masks, caps, gloves, and goggles.

2. Which sentence means the same thing as the following sentence? "As he read, a chill must have gone down his spine."

☐ a. It was quite cold in the room where he was reading.

☐ b. What he read must have frightened him.

☐ c. While he was reading, he started to feel chills and fever.

Score 4 points for each correct answer.

_____ **Total Score:** Summarizing and Paraphrasing

G. Critical Thinking

Put an X in the box next to the correct answer.

1. Choose the statement below that states an opinion.

☐ a. It was good that Dr. Matthew worked from early morning until late at night for many weeks.

☐ b. Goggles that protected the doctors and nurses also made it harder for them to do their jobs.

☐ c. Victims of Ebola virus coughed up blood and got nosebleeds.

2. From information in the article, you can predict that

☐ a. no one else at St. Mary's Hospital will be willing to work with Ebola victims again.

☐ b. no one will ever find a cure for the Ebola virus.

☐ c. Dr. Matthew's wife and children are proud of him.

3. The 2000-2001 Ebola outbreak in Gulu and other Ebola outbreaks were different because

☐ a. many people died in the Gulu outbreak, but no one died in the others.

☐ b. the death rate was lower in Gulu than in the other outbreaks.

☐ c. no one died in Gulu, but many died in other outbreaks.

4. Which paragraph provides information that supports your answer to question 3?

☐ a. paragraph 5

☐ b. paragraph 6

☐ c. paragraph 12

5. Which lesson about life does this story teach?

☐ a. Sometimes we have to do what is best for others, not for ourselves.

☐ b. Everything that is natural is good for human beings.

☐ c. Modern science can cure any disease.

Score 4 points for each correct answer.

_____ **Total Score:** Critical Thinking

Enter your score for each activity. Add the scores together. Record your total score on the graph on page 115.

_____ Finding the Main Idea

_____ Recalling Facts

_____ Making Inferences

_____ Using Words

_____ Author's Approach

_____ Summarizing and Paraphrasing

_____ Critical Thinking

_____ **Total Score**

Personal Response

Would you tell other students to read this article? Explain.

_____

_____

Self-Assessment

From reading this article, I have learned _____

_____

_____

Racing Through the Pain

Kristina Strode-Penny was tough. In fact, she was so tough people began calling her "Xena, the Warrior Princess." Strode-Penny competed in one of the hardest sports in the world. She was an adventure racer. Adventure races don't last just an hour or two. They go on for days. They combine running, biking, rafting, and kayaking. That by itself makes them rugged. But to add to the challenge, adventure races cover some of the roughest parts of the world. So they might take racers through deserts, mountains, or jungles.

2   Strode-Penny grew up in New Zealand. She loved the outdoor life. As a young girl, she climbed mountains. She learned to mountain bike, and she loved to run. Her family lived near the sea. So she also learned to propel a kayak, which is a type of canoe. In time, Strode-Penny took up adventure racing. "Adventure racing seemed to put all the skills I had learned together," she said.

3   Strode-Penny soon became one of the best racers anywhere. She won one race by more than a day. But

Shown here is the New Zealand team on day six of the Eco-Challenge adventure race held on the island nation of Fiji.

things did not always go that well. In one five-day race, she lasted just 16 hours. In another, she was bucked off the back of a horse and broke both ankles.

4   In 2002 Strode-Penny joined a team from New Zealand called Seagate. The team had four members—Strode-Penny and three men. Their goal was to win the Eco-Challenge held on the island nation of Fiji. The race covered more than 300 miles. It was almost like a contest against nature itself. The course was filled with mountains and jungles and swift rivers. The race would be the ultimate test for the 81 teams entered. The names of its sections hinted at what the racers would face. One section was called Trail of Fire. Another was Valley of Pain. Adventure racers don't usually die, but they often get so sick or so tired they might wish they were dead.

5   In Fiji, Seagate got off to a slow start. Like the other teams, they were given 13 bamboo poles and some cord. With those, they had to make a raft. Then they had to paddle 25 miles down a river. Most teams, including Seagate, struggled. But one team had practiced making rafts. They quickly took the lead.

6   After leaving the river, the racers had to cut their way through the steamy jungle. They used large, sharp blades to cut down the trees and vines in their way. In one area, the vines were so thick it took an hour to

travel 200 yards. The racers also had to scramble up waterfalls and trudge through mud. By the third day, Seagate had to stop. Strode-Penny was in bad shape. She was vomiting constantly. Worse, the heat was getting to her. Her fever was so high that she couldn't drink water. Teammate Jeff Mitchell had to pour cold water over her head to help cool her down.

7   For a team to win, all four members have to cross the finish line. So Seagate couldn't go on until Strode-Penny got stronger. Most teams don't sleep more than an hour in any 24-hour period. But because of Strode-Penny, Seagate rested 10 hours in the first three days. They hadn't planned to do it. But it turned out to be a blessing in disguise. According to Jeff Mitchell, "It was the reason we won."

8   As a result of their long breaks, Seagate was better rested than any other team. They were far behind the leaders, but they had the energy to move quickly. They passed one team after another. On the fifth day, they flew past GoLite, the team that had won in 2001. "They were moving so fast they dropped our jaws," said GoLite's Michael Kloser.

9   Now there was just one team ahead of them, a Spanish team called Buff AXN. By this time, two members of Buff AXN had terrible foot problems. They couldn't walk, and so their team had to quit. Seagate sprinted to the lead and won the race. They had completed the course in six days and 23 hours. GoLite, in second place, finished six hours behind them.

10   In all, only 23 of the 81 teams made it to the finish line. All the others dropped out. Some suffered injuries, and a few were simply worn out. But most, like Buff AXN, struggled with severe foot troubles. Some racers cut their feet in river beds. Some racers could not walk at all because their feet became so swollen.

11   As it turned out, Strode-Penny had not escaped these dangers. At some point in the race, parasites got into her body. Most likely these tiny worms got under her skin when she had her socks off. In the days following the race, Strode-Penny became weaker and weaker. The worms left her with no energy. Her doctors tried everything to get rid of them. Nothing worked.

12   At last doctors offered her a medicine usually only given to sheep. By then Strode-Penny was willing to try anything. So she took it. The medicine worked. After just three days, the parasites were gone. Strode-Penny was soon much better. By the spring of 2003, she was back in top form. As she set off on her next race, it was easy to see why one reporter called her "the world's leading female adventure racer."

A. Finding the Main Idea

One statement below tells the main idea of the article. One statement is too general, or too broad. The other statement explains only part of the article; it is too narrow. Label the statements using the following key:

M—Main Idea   B—Too Broad   N—Too Narrow

_____ 1. In 2002 Kristina Strode-Penny was part of a team called Seagate. As the team raced through the jungles of Fiji, she became quite sick. She started vomiting and had a high fever.

_____ 2. Kristina Strode-Penny may be the best female adventure racer in the world. Though she got sick during a 2002 race in Fiji and slowed her team down, the team won the race anyway.

_____ 3. Adventure racing is a tough sport. It puts racers in dangerous places and asks them to do difficult tasks. To compete in adventure races, athletes must be strong and fearless.

Score 4 points for each correct answer.

_____ **Total Score:** Finding the Main Idea

B. Recalling Facts

How well do you remember the facts in the article? Put an X in the box next to the answer that correctly completes each statement.

1. Kristina Strode-Penny grew up in
   ☐ a. the United States.
   ☐ b. New Zealand.
   ☐ c. South Africa.

2. In the 2002 Eco-Challenge in Fiji, the Seagate team had
   ☐ a. four members.
   ☐ b. six members.
   ☐ c. eight members.

3. Strode-Penny's team didn't go on without her when she became ill because
   ☐ a. all the rest of the team members were sick too.
   ☐ b. none of the other members really cared about winning.
   ☐ c. all four members had to cross the finish line.

4. Parasites are
   ☐ a. tiny worms that can get into a person's body.
   ☐ b. special tools that adventure racers use to get through jungles.
   ☐ c. medicines that doctors gave Strode-Penny at the end of the Eco-Challenge.

Score 4 points for each correct answer.

_____ **Total Score:** Recalling Facts

C. Making Inferences

When you draw a conclusion that is not directly stated in the text, you are making an inference. Put an X in the box next to the statement that is a correct inference.

1.

☐ a. Doctors are always on hand to help if anyone gets sick during the Eco-Challenge.

☐ b. It is rare that racers become so sick or injured during an adventure race that they have to quit.

☐ c. To win an adventure race, you must be good at several different sports.

2.

☐ a. In the end, the other members of Seagate were glad that Strode-Penny had forced them to rest 10 hours in the first three days.

☐ b. Strode-Penny is not a person who is willing to take chances with unusual medicines.

☐ c. People who set up the 2002 Eco-Challenge course in Fiji did not think it would be very difficult.

Score 4 points for each correct answer.

_____ **Total Score:** Making Inferences

D. Using Words

Put an X in the box next to the definition below that is closest in meaning to the underlined word.

1. The course was so rugged that only a few athletes completed it.

☐ a. short
☐ b. difficult
☐ c. easy

2. Everyone is supposed to come to the Halloween party in disguise. I am going as a knight in armor.

☐ a. an old-fashioned type of carriage
☐ b. a way of acting that makes you look rich
☐ c. clothes or ways of acting that hide who you are

3. Some people say the ultimate challenge for an athlete is hiking up the world's tallest mountain, Mount Everest.

☐ a. greatest
☐ b. funniest
☐ c. weakest

4. After a sudden storm, the hikers had to trudge through knee-high snow for hours.

☐ a. skip happily
☐ b. walk slowly, in a tired way
☐ c. run lightly, with plenty of energy

5. The little boy behind me at the movies was <u>constantly</u> kicking the back of my seat, so I asked him to stop.

☐ a. without pausing
☐ b. hardly ever
☐ c. never again

6. Juan was tired but, to everyone's surprise, he <u>sprinted</u> to the finish line and won the race.

☐ a. threw a ball
☐ b. walked slowly
☐ c. ran fast

Score 4 points for each correct answer.

_____ **Total Score:** Using Words

E. Author's Approach

Put an X in the box next to the correct answer.

1. The main purpose of the first paragraph is to

☐ a. compare adventure racing and mountain climbing.
☐ b. describe both Strode-Penny and adventure racing.
☐ c. explain why Strode-Penny started competing in adventure races.

2. From the statements below, choose the one that you believe the author would agree with.

☐ a. Strode-Penny is a person who complains a lot when things don't go her way.
☐ b. Strode-Penny usually gets lucky breaks during her races.
☐ c. Strode-Penny is especially good at what she does.

3. Choose the statement below that is the weakest argument for entering an adventure race.

☐ a. When you compete in an adventure race, you have a chance to make new friends.
☐ b. Competing in an adventure race could help you prove to yourself that you are strong and brave.
☐ c. You could become sick or injured during an adventure race.

Score 4 points for each correct answer.

_____ **Total Score:** Author's Approach

F. Summarizing and Paraphrasing

Put an X in the box next to the correct answer.

1. Which summary says all the important things about the article?

☐ a. Adventure racer Kristina Strode-Penny accepts the dangers that come with competing in tough, days-long races. In one race, she overcame sickness to help her team win. She got better and soon went back to racing.

☐ b. Kristina Strode-Penny grew up near the ocean. That is why she is so good at water sports. She also does well at other sports that are part of adventure racing.

☐ c. In an Eco-Challenge race in Fiji, many teams had trouble. Seagate had to rest for hours because one member was sick. Other teams suffered from foot problems or became so tired they couldn't move fast.

2. Which sentence means the same thing as the following sentence? "They were moving so fast they dropped our jaws."

☐ a. Moving that fast would have hurt our jaws.

☐ b. We were amazed at how quickly they were moving.

☐ c. As they moved past quickly, they bumped our jaws.

Score 4 points for each correct answer.

_____ **Total Score:** Summarizing and Paraphrasing

G. Critical Thinking

Put an X in the box next to the correct answer.

1. Choose the statement below that states an opinion.

☐ a. The 2003 Eco-Challenge race course in Fiji covered over 300 miles.

☐ b. Everyone who is young and healthy should compete in an adventure race.

☐ c. The team called Buff AXN had to quit the Eco-Challenge because two members couldn't walk.

2. From information in the article, you can predict that

☐ a. Strode-Penny will probably keep competing in adventure races as long as she can.

☐ b. Strode-Penny will soon decide that adventure races are too dangerous and will work to make them illegal.

☐ c. no other athletes will ever ask Strode-Penny to be on their adventure race teams.

3. Seagate and Buff AXN are different because

☐ a. only Seagate ran into problems during the race.

☐ b. only members of Buff AXN were from New Zealand.

☐ c. only Seagate won the 2002 Eco-Challenge.

4. How is Kristina Strode-Penny an example of someone who goes into the danger zone?

☐ a. She is good at many sports.

☐ b. She competes in races that could hurt her.

☐ c. She once had parasites and had to take medicine to get rid of them.

5. If you were an adventure racer, how could you use the information in the article to win a race?

☐ a. Like Strode-Penny, I would get enough rest so I could finish the race strong.

☐ b. I would ignore my sickness or injury and travel until I was completely exhausted.

☐ c. When I put together my team, I would not choose anyone who might get tired, sick, or hurt.

Score 4 points for each correct answer.

_____ **Total Score:** Critical Thinking

Enter your score for each activity. Add the scores together. Record your total score on the graph on page 115.

_____ Finding the Main Idea

_____ Recalling Facts

_____ Making Inferences

_____ Using Words

_____ Author's Approach

_____ Summarizing and Paraphrasing

_____ Critical Thinking

_____ **Total Score**

Personal Response

I know the feeling _____

_____

_____

Self-Assessment

One good question about this article that was not asked would be "_____

_____

_____ ?"

Compare and Contrast

Pick two stories in Unit Three that tell about people who became sick or hurt on the job or while taking part in a sport. Use information from the stories to fill in this chart.

Title	What was the person doing when he or she became sick or hurt?	Describe the sickness or injury.	Did this person continue doing the job or sport? Why or why not?

Which of these people seems most like you? Explain why you chose him or her. _____

_____

_____

Comprehension and Critical Thinking Progress Graph

Directions: Write your score for each lesson in the box under the number of the lesson.
Then put a small X on the line directly above the number of the lesson and across from
the score you earned. Chart your progress by drawing a line to connect the Xs.

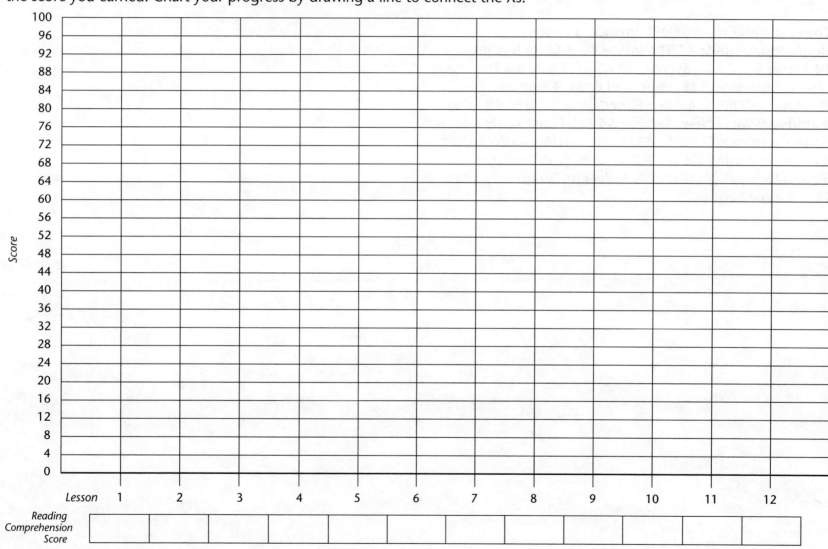

Photo Credits

Cover